NEW HARMONY THEN & NOW

New Harmony Then & Now

TEXT *Donald E. Pitzer*   PHOTOGRAPHS *Darryl D. Jones*   FOREWORD *Jane Blaffer Owen & Connie Weinzapfel*

QUARRY BOOKS   *an imprint of*   INDIANA UNIVERSITY PRESS   *Bloomington & Indianapolis*

This book is a publication of

QUARRY BOOKS

an imprint of

INDIANA UNIVERSITY PRESS
601 North Morton Street
Bloomington, Indiana 47404–3797 USA

iupress.indiana.edu

Telephone orders   800-842-6796
Fax orders   812-855-7931
Orders by e-mail   iuporder@indiana.edu

∞ The paper used in this publication meets the minimum requirements of the American National Standard for Information Sciences—Permanence of Paper for Printed Library Materials, ANSI Z39.48–1992.

Manufactured in China

Library of Congress
Cataloging-in-Publication Data

Pitzer, Donald E.
  New Harmony then and now / text by Donald E. Pitzer ; photographs by Darryl D. Jones ; foreword by Jane Blaffer Owen and Connie Weinzapfel.
     p. cm. — (Quarry books)
  Includes bibliographical references and index.
  ISBN 978-0-253-35645-1 (cloth : alk. paper) 1. New Harmony (Ind.)—History. 2. New Harmony (Ind.)—Pictorial works. 3. Harmony Society. 4. Collective settlements—Indiana—New Harmony—History. I. Jones, Darryl, 1948- II. Title.
  HX656.N5P58   2011
  307.7709772'34—dc23   2011025278

1 2 3 4 5   16 15 14 13 12 11

It is wholly appropriate that this book is dedicated to the spirit of Jane Blaffer Owen. Many of the places so beautifully captured here were reborn or given life by her. In the lush landscapes, elegant architecture, and the faces of the people, one sees a tribute to her dedication to this community. She spent nearly seventy years pulling the ideals of our past into the moment. This moment in New Harmony's long history is hers.

CONNIE WEINZAPFEL

For my wife, Connie Pitzer, and for my granddaughter, Harmony Dove Malie Pitzer, my hope for New Harmony's utopian promise.

DONALD E. PITZER

To my wife, Nancy; our son Aaron; our daughter Hannah and son-in-law Ben O'Connor and their daughter Fiona Rose;
the memory of my parents, William B. and Edna Jones, Jr.; my grandparents; and our relatives in Posey County.

DARRYL D. JONES

CONTENTS

FOREWORD

BORN OF THE MIDCONTINENT WETLANDS on the New World frontier, New Harmony moves through time like the slow, low meandering ribbon of its Wabash River in August.

This village, this town, this place, this state of mind called New Harmony, was built by Swabian pilgrims following their religious leader into a land of plenty. As true believers, the Harmonie Society toiled to provide physical, spiritual, and intellectual abundance for its members. A decade later, Robert Owen and those he attracted to his Community of Equality brought with them the desire to raise up the working classes to a higher level of opportunity, as demanded in a democracy.

Owen and his partner, William Maclure, brought their retinue and came with arms open, ready to give, for the improvement of humanity. Innovations in social theory, educational systems, and discoveries in the natural sciences distinguished New Harmony throughout the United States and, indeed, throughout the world. Owen's great social experiment could not endure, but the new social frontier flourished.

As the nineteenth and twentieth centuries flowed into history, so too did New Harmony. Still a small village raising the lantern of promise for the future, the town preserved its progressive core. Brilliant minds and industrious souls are drawn to this *thin* place.

Some visit and some settle. At this moment, New Harmony is closer to realizing the complementary aspirations of its communal founders, balancing science and spirit.

As we approach New Harmony's bicentennial, let us find inspiration from those who came before—the Woodland natives who lived by and safeguarded nature's bounty; the entrepreneurship of the fervent Germans who founded and built the town; the Enlightenment idealism of Owen and Maclure, their families and followers.

From the Greek, *utopia* means "no place"—never to be in actuality, but always to be in the soul of New Harmony.

JANE BLAFFER OWEN
Robert Lee Blaffer Foundation, New Harmony

CONNIE WEINZAPFEL
Historic New Harmony, a unified program
of the University of Southern Indiana and the
Indiana State Museum and Historic Sites

PREFACE

MANY BOOKS HAVE BEEN WRITTEN about the legendary New Harmony, Indiana, but this is the first to combine its utopian past with its illustrious present. In words and images, this book brings New Harmony's ideas, people, and beauty to life in a single volume. Darryl Jones and I have joined our areas of expertise in this effort: his in photography and mine in communal utopian history.

The result is a work we hope will be enjoyed by visitors, residents, and other readers with a broad range of interests. New Harmony both then and now has spanned an impressive spectrum of human endeavor that continues to connect it vitally with the wider world and to attract national and international attention. Ever since the days of its Harmonist and Owenite founders, in the early nineteenth century, this little town has been an arena for wrestling with the ultimate universal questions of life and existence, of spirituality and science, and of the secret of happiness. Our book invites those who would experience the wonder produced by free people in a free land exercising their freedom of mind, body, and spirit into this labyrinth of the unusual and amazing, of utopians and experimenters, of inventors and builders.

Fortunately, many people and institutions have appreciated the heritage which is New Harmony and have contributed generously to its physical, intellectual, and spiritual preservation and its present vitality. With photographs and descriptions, this book features these unique structures, events, and qualities. The Working Men's Institute, established by funds from William Maclure in 1838, continues as the oldest working library in the state. Murphy Auditorium thrives as a theatrical center, having begun with an original gift from Dr. Edward Murphy and his wife, Sophia, in 1900. Thrall's Opera House, a former Harmonist dormitory, is the scene of plays, galas, and balls. The reconstructed Harmonist hedge labyrinth entices visitors into its circles.

The Robert Lee Blaffer Foundation, established in honor of the father of New Harmony's late patron Jane Blaffer Owen, and the Lilly Endowment have been responsible for numerous modern projects of physical preservation and cultural enrichment. In this book, their and others' philanthropic projects come to life. The Roofless Church, designed by Philip Johnson, provides a favorite venue for weddings. The Atheneum Visitors Center, designed by Richard Meier, offers exhibits and tours. Adaptively restored, the massive Rapp Granary–David Dale Owen Laboratory accommodates large groups for professional and public meetings. An interpretation of the Chartres Cathedral labyrinth complements the rebuilt one of the Harmonists.

Historic New Harmony, a unified program of the University of Southern Indiana and the Indiana State Museum and Historic Sites, oversees historic properties, operates the visitors center, maintains an archive, and facilitates educational and other public events. The University of Southern Indiana in nearby Evansville has a Center for Communal Studies in its School of Liberal Arts and a Communal Studies Collection in the Special Collections Department of its David L. Rice Library, both of which work to foster scholarly activity in and about New Harmony.

All who are interested in New Harmony are grateful that it, the other two Harmonist settlements, and Robert Owen's Scottish mill town have received significant attention for physical and archival preservation and program development. Each can be toured on-site and online: New Harmony at www.usi.edu/hnh; Harmony, Pennsylvania, at www.harmony-pa.us; Old Economy Village at Ambridge, Pennsylvania, at www.oldeconomyvillage .org; and Robert Owen's historic New Lanark, Scotland, a World Heritage Site, at www.newlanark.org.

In the production of this volume, Darryl Jones and I are deeply indebted to all those who have preserved New Harmony, its buildings and grounds, and its archival resources and traditions over the years. A short list includes Helen Elliott, John and Josephine Elliott, Don Blair, Kenneth Dale and Jane Blaffer Owen, Jim Sanders, Eberhard and Ruth Reichmann, and David and Betty Rice, but there are hundreds more. To all who personally assisted us in the research, writing, photography, and creation of this volume, we also express our gratitude. Among these are Connie Weinzapfel, Jan Kahle, Amanda Bryden, and Christine Crews of Historic New Harmony; Sherry Graves of the Working Men's Institute; Jennifer Greene and Deanna Engler of the University of Southern Indiana library; Mary Ann Landis, Sarah Buffington, and Holly Dofner of Old Economy Village; Lorna Davidson of the New Lanark Trust; Pat Brandwood of the Robert Owen Museum in Newtown, Wales; and Linda Oblack and other members of the editorial staff of Indiana University Press.

DONALD E. PITZER
Professor Emeritus of History
Director Emeritus, Center for Communal Studies
University of Southern Indiana
Evansville, Indiana
November 2010

MY IMMEDIATE RELATIONSHIP with New Harmony began on my paternal side in Posey County, Indiana. My father's mother, Katherine Deuischer, came with her family from Baden-Baden, Germany, and settled along the Ohio River at Mount Vernon. My father was born there in 1914, one hundred years after the Rappites moved to New Harmony, and his grade school classes would often have trips to visit and learn about New Harmony. Though my father's family moved to Terre Haute and then to Fort Wayne, where I was born and grew up, we would often make the long drive from northeast to extreme southwest Indiana to visit relatives. We would sometimes meet at a farm that belonged to my father's cousin and bordered the Ohio River near Hovey Lake.

The farmhouse was stained to the ceiling from the great 1937 flood, and I saw photographs of my relatives Lola and Lloyd Deuischer escaping from the second floor into a rowboat. During our visits we would take a ferry across the Ohio River and return to follow the Ohio to the confluence of the Wabash and Ohio Rivers. These early experiences provided lasting impressions of the way of life along the Wabash and Ohio that would influence my desire to document the town of New Harmony.

My first visit to New Harmony was not until 1982. A year earlier, I had begun a book project to photograph Indiana. I produced photographic images in all ninety-two counties, and in Posey County I concentrated on New Harmony, Mount Vernon, and Hovey Lake. In New Harmony I knew that I wanted to see the first U.S. Geological Laboratory, founded by David Dale Owen. Since this was a privately owned building, I needed to obtain permission to visit and take photographs. Tina Conner of the Historic Landmarks Foundation of Indiana arranged a fortuitous meeting for me with Jane Owen of New Harmony. Jane graciously gave me permission and encouraged the whole endeavor, predicting that one day I would do a book on New Harmony.

When the book *Indiana* came out in 1984, the photograph of the David Dale Owen Laboratory appeared as a large double-page spread. Jane Owen loved that photograph and arranged a book signing at the Red Geranium bookstore. Concurrently, I had an exhibit and program at the Atheneum. Jane invited me to dinner and to attend the opera at Thrall's Opera. She treated me the way she treated all authors, artists, and guests—with great hospitality. I would not see Jane for another two decades.

In 2006 I began to photograph New Harmony, and I started with Kunstfest. The first person I met was a distinguished woman wearing a simple blue dress and a hat with a wide brim. It was Jane Owen, and we reacted to each other as old friends. Although we had not met in twenty-two years, she began our conversation exactly where we left off. She said that she would often tell my story of my 1971 visit to the home of Mary, mother of Jesus, in Ephesus, Turkey. What impressed her most was my description of hundreds of Turkish women who went there on a pilgrimage and stayed the entire day in prayer and contemplation, returning home with holy water to heal the sick. This, for me, was a firsthand experience of the spirituality of another religion.

After continuing travels in Turkey, Greece, and Italy, I returned to graduate school at Indiana University in 1972, studying the sacred scriptures of many religions and their saints who had interpreted those scriptures mystically. Jane loved hearing about this, because interfaith dialogue was extremely important to her, and she viewed New Harmony as a sacred place where that dialogue could occur in a peaceful setting. Thus our conversation continued as she invited me to have lunch at her Harmonist home and meet other scholars and poets. Jane wholeheartedly encouraged me about the new book project on New Harmony. During the next three years I would see her and tell her of the book's progress. While she did not live to see its publication, she had an influential role as the spiritual support of this project.

DARRYL DEUISCHER JONES
Freedom, Indiana
May 2011

NEW HARMONY

Then & Now

THEN

NEW HARMONY'S UTOPIAN HERITAGE

VISUALIZE A VILLAGE on the Indiana frontier so innovative and controversial it became internationally famous in the early nineteenth century. Conceive a community founded by a thousand celibate German immigrants to await the Second Coming of Christ. Picture a place purchased by a wealthy textile mill owner from Scotland who attracted nationally known educators and scientists to create a New Moral World.

This is the utopian heritage of New Harmony on the Wabash. The radical ideas, social innovations, and scientific findings of two idealistic movements—one religious, the other secular—brought New Harmony, Indiana, the attention of the Western world: First came George Rapp's Harmonists, who built the town from 1814 to 1824; second were Robert Owen's Owenites, who converted its 180 buildings to serve their own communal experiment from 1825 to 1827.

Two of the most potent ideas in modern history brought these utopians into the wilderness: millennialism and socialism. Both promised a world of peace and plenty. Millennialism offered hope for the return of Christ and the establishment of a Kingdom of God on earth. George Rapp convinced his disciples that signs in nature and human affairs foretold that this prophetic event was imminent. Socialism, in the humanitarian form conceived by Robert Owen, guaranteed social equality and happiness through education, science, and communal living, in the end transforming human character itself. His New Harmony was to be the first working model.

Preparing for their millennial utopia inspired the Harmonists to build three towns, create a business empire, and influence early political developments in Indiana and the nation. Pursuing their humanitarian goals in the name of socialism made the Owenites leaders for public schools, libraries, museums, scientific discovery, trade unions, freedom for slaves, and equal rights for women.

HARMONIST GERMAN ORIGINS (1757–1803)

Nearly sixty years before New Harmony burst upon international consciousness, the prophet of the Harmonist movement, George Rapp, was born Johann Georg Rapp on November 1, 1757.[1] Iptingen, his hometown, was northwest of Stuttgart in the Swabian Duchy of Württemberg. Disturbing undercurrents flowed beneath the tranquil surface of the little village in which George Rapp grew to manhood although it looked right out of a fairy tale—as it still does today. The undercurrents ran as far back as the Protestant Reformation. They created a flood of physical and emotional suffering that eventually carried thousands of distraught peasants toward Rapp's safe harbor of spiritual solace and anticipation of Christ's prompt return. Ever since the sixteenth century, Württemberg had been caught up in the turbulent warfare caused by religious and political controversy. The Peasant War began in the German provinces in 1524 and took a hundred thousand lives across Europe in two years. In the Thirty Years' War, from 1618 to 1648, Lutherans, Calvinists, and Roman Catholics battled to dominate the European continent. Württemberg survived the carnage and the pillage of mercenaries as a Lutheran stronghold but lay in shambles at war's end, having lost three-quarters of its population.

As widespread economic hardship, famine, disease, and death intensified the need for heart-felt comfort from their faith, Württembergers found Lutheranism increasingly intellectualized and rationalistic, its services coldly formal and devoted to ritual. For decades many sought healing for body, mind, and spirit beyond the established church. Some began reading and illegally interpreting the Bible for themselves. Others went beyond the acceptable writings of Martin Luther to embrace the soothing but extreme doctrines of radical pietists and mystical speculators, including alchemists. Wave after wave of believers were driven into outright religious dissent and separatism, criminal acts against the state as well as the church in Lutheran Württemberg.

Such troubled waters pushed the young George Rapp in the same perilous direction. After he lost the security and guidance of his father, Hans Adam Rapp, at age fourteen, his inquisitive mind and leadership qualities, including a six-foot frame and a commanding voice, led him into the depths of religious radicalism. He first became a philosophical seeker, then a convincing dissenter, and finally the magnetic prophet of one of the largest separatist groups to leave the established Lutheran Church and escape to the religious freedom of America.

In 1783, he married Christina Benzinger, who shared his dangerous religious views. They illegally lured separatists from the established Lutheran Church and rooted their faith in what can be simplified as four Ps and a C: pietism, an emotional conversion experience and personal relationship with God; perfectionism, a goal that eventually demanded celibacy; pacifism, peaceful resolution of disputes and refusal to serve in the military; and postmillennialism, the optimistic idea that progress in human nature and human affairs was preparing the world for Christ's return. To these early tenets of the Harmonist movement, Rapp later added only one: Christian communalism, based on the community of goods practiced by the first-century congregation of Peter in Jerusalem and described in Acts 2 and 4.

From Martin Luther, the founder of the very Lutheranism whose corruption Rapp now scorned, the budding prophet retained justification by faith alone and the priesthood of all believers. However, he enhanced these often neglected doctrines with a pietistic emphasis that assured the common people of their right to the direct communion with God they so desperately sought. He had first immersed himself in the original wellspring of pietism among seventeenth-century German theologians and scholars, especially the theologian Philipp Spener, considered the "Father of Pietism," and the professor August Francke. From the radical pietism of his contemporary, Johann Heinrich Jung-Stilling, Rapp understood salvation to be contingent upon a personal spiritual rebirth, which he claimed to have experienced in 1785.

That same year, young Rapp the dissenter became Rapp the radical separatist, breaking with the established Lutheran Church and ending sexual relations with his wife after siring two children, Johann (John) and Rosina. He took the perfectionist step of sexual self-denial for two reasons: to reach toward pietism's demand for

George Rapp.

Courtesy of the State Museum of Pennsylvania, Pennsylvania Historical and Museum Commission.

Evangelical Lutheran Church, Iptingen, Germany, 1974

Photo by Donald Pitzer.

Christian perfection and to emulate a claim of German mystic Jacob Boehme that Adam lived fully in the image of God only before his dual sexuality was separated into female and male like the animals, thus permitting sin to enter the Garden of Eden. After 1785, celibacy became the ideal for Rapp's disciples and, after 1807, the rule.

At an early age, George Rapp gained great respect from disciples who were in awe of their tall, oratorically gifted, black-dressed, and black-bearded sage. By 1809, they were calling him "Father."[2] But his status among the dissenters of Württemberg gave him no protection from charges of blasphemy when he challenged the church by personally interpreting scripture, or from imprisonment when he preached his heresies publicly and thereby fomented civil unrest. He had gone so far as to condone his separatists' disrespectfully driving their pigs by the Lutheran church during Sunday morning services. His outspoken attacks upon the corruption of the church and upon military service to the state could not go unnoticed or unpunished even in relatively tolerant Württemberg. From 1785 to 1803, Father Rapp and his separatist movement, which eventually was as many as twelve thousand strong, fought a running battle with both clerical and civil authorities. Each side knew it was in a tug-of-war: the separatists wanting their freedom of worship but not wanting to be jailed or exiled; the church and civil authorities not wanting to lose parishioners and citizens but wanting to enforce dogma and law.

In 1785, the Iptingen Church Council called the twenty-eight-year-old upstart to answer for absenting himself from services. By 1787, the church had launched a series of investigations to discover just how threatening his unorthodox ideas and growing band of believers had become. George and Christina Rapp and a dozen other separatists were the first questioned. When asked for a written confession of faith, George explained his path to a personal relationship with Jesus Christ. In all humility, he said, this conver-

sion negated his need for baptism, confirmation, and Holy Communion in any organized church.

By the time these disturbing results were forwarded to the Württemberg Lutheran Synod and the civil court in Maulbronn, Rapp had become scornful and condescending. Charged with calling church members hypocrites, the Lutheran Lord's Supper blasphemous, and Sunday a Jewish feast, he argued that only he and his followers understood the scriptures and that the clergy were not qualified to be pastors without a spiritual rebirth—something their university education did not guarantee. In 1791, when the judicial decision was read in court—a stern warning, a threat of exile, and imprisonment for two days—Rapp dared raise his voice in protest. As the government official commanded him to be silent, taunting him that he was no prophet, Rapp retorted with a bold, if not treasonable, proclamation: "I am a prophet and am called to be one!"

Prophet Rapp's brief incarceration gave him a martyr's influence while leaving him alive to expand the very movement which the civil authorities had hoped to quell. Fearing that creating an atmosphere of recrimination might cause another Peasant War, Duke Karl Eugen not only rejected the synod's recommendation of immediate exile but also urged the local clergy to ignore the self-proclaimed prophet. The unintended result was a ten-year lull in which Rapp's stature and disruptive movement grew to unacceptable proportions.

Rapp inflamed the hearts and minds of thousands in his own hometown, in neighboring villages, and throughout southwest Germany. Deliberately, he proselytized Lutheran parishioners, often setting them in bitter opposition to their families, friends, and clergy, who then pressured reluctant civil authorities to censor Rapp's movement. In the next investigation, in 1798, the Reform Württemberg Legislature required Rapp and his separatist lead-

ers to summarize their articles of faith. These articles recounted the biblical foundation for the separatists' radical brand of piety: their imitation of primitive Christianity, including its Holy Communion for bona fide believers only, and their opposition to infant baptism, confirmation, taking oaths, military service, and exposing their children to Lutheran-polluted public schools. The reform legislature might have looked kindly enough upon the Rappites to offer them legal status, but the new, less tolerant duke, Frederick II, dismissed that body before any action could be taken.

After the irritating separatist from Iptingen spoke to three overflow meetings in Kittlingen, he was commanded never again to preach outside his hometown and was summoned to give another personal testimony in Maulbronn. There, in April 1802, when he blatantly referred to himself as the bishop of what amounted to the separatist Rappite Church, he knew that if he confined his ministry to his hometown his prophetic mission would be over and if he did not he could be exiled. He also felt the deep emotions aroused among his pacifists when Duke Frederick made military service a top priority as the French Revolution branched into war. Many feared Frederick would even revive Duke Eugen's hated policy of selling Germans as mercenaries to other powers. Rapp's faithful were primed to emigrate. They would choose the nightmare of leaving their beloved ancestral homes to that of being forced to participate in bloodshed.

Millennialism was the key to Rapp's power over his flock. The comforting and inspiring belief that the Messiah will return has periodically held center stage in the Christian world. Prophecies and Jesus's promises guarantee it. Signs and wonders portend it. Jung-Stilling and Johann Gottfried Herder, another prominent German theologian and philosopher of Rapp's era, strongly influenced him with their evidence of developments that signaled the imminence of Christ's return.[3] They inspired Rapp to interpret prophecies for himself. Using millennialism as the engine to drive the urgency of all his teachings, he skillfully interpreted biblical passages to mean that his Harmonists were God's chosen people for the end-times, the true spiritual Israel and the Bride of Christ. They were the favored church of Philadelphia in Revelation 3. And, above all, they were the prophetic Sunwoman of Revelation 12—the woman clothed with the sun who begets the millennial Christ and flees from Satan into the wilderness. Rapp set his Harmonist movement apart from all other millennialists by asserting that his purified saints alone represented this soon-to-be-fulfilled prophecy. The explanation of everything else the Harmonists did hinges upon this conviction that they must play this vital role of the Sunwoman before Christ could return. The concept of fleeing into the wilderness inspired their emigration to America.

Since millennial prophesies have the convenient quality of being evident in most any age, Rapp found it easy to convince himself and his disciples that world events were pointing in this utopian direction, especially as described in the books of Daniel and Revelation. The French Revolution of 1789 became another step in the purification of human social and political institutions in preparation for Christ's kingdom on earth. In the eyes of Rapp and other millennialists, Napoleon Bonaparte became a messenger from heaven, a forerunner for Christ's return if not a second son of God, sent to crush the corrupt Catholic and Lutheran churches. The fall of these false churches would alert the faithful that Christ's return was at hand. By 1802, Rapp felt under such duress at home that he wrote to Napoleon requesting permission to settle in French Louisiana with an estimated 1,200 separatists. Although permission was granted, Napoleon sold Louisiana to the United States before Rapp, like a Swabian Moses, could lead his people to their promised land.[4] In the summer of 1803, accompanied by his son, John, and two close friends, he fled his German homeland for

the rights and freedoms of the new United States of America. In all, this prophet from Iptingen would induce more than two thousand Wüttembergers to cross an ocean and build three towns in the frontier wilderness of Pennsylvania and Indiana. This became one of the largest religious migrations to the United States under the leadership of a single individual.

THE HARMONY SOCIETY AT HARMONY, PENNSYLVANIA (1803–1814)

Once he arrived in Philadelphia on October 7, George Rapp's first mission was to secure sufficient land in one place for settling the thousands he had every reason to believe would follow him to the New World. He needed cheap, arable land on a long-term loan. A yearlong search took him away from the most desirable locations along the eastern seaboard to the wilds of western Pennsylvania and Ohio. Eventually, his tiresome quest led him to a personal meeting with President Thomas Jefferson on July 12, 1804. Rapp hoped to obtain special terms for buying as much as forty thousand acres (nearly two townships) on the Muskingum River in the new state of Ohio. He wanted to pay less than the regular $2 per acre for government land or, at least, to be excused the one-quarter down payment in cash and be allowed more than the usual four years to pay in full. Always bold, the Harmonist leader made clear his utopian plans and land requests. Jefferson received the German prophet and his intentions kindly but explained that the president of a republic, unlike the duke of a duchy, did not have the power to alter the law on purchasing public land. In 1806, a request to purchase a whole township, twenty-three thousand acres, near Vincennes in the Indiana Territory was approved by the U.S. Senate. However, the vote in the House of Representatives was a tie decided in the negative by Speaker Nathaniel Macon—

after many complimented the Harmonists' piety and morality but objected to the prospect of having foreigners establish themselves in an exclusive community within American territory or of selling prime land to outsiders on favorable terms not available to United States citizens.[5]

In the meantime, hundreds of Rapp's disciples had crossed the Atlantic. The first boatload providentially landed in Baltimore on July 4, 1804. July Fourth became an annual day of feasting for the Harmonists as much to commemorate this arrival as to celebrate American independence. Shipload by shipload, Rapp's immigrant flock rapidly increased beyond one thousand. His three sisters made the crossing and his only brother lost his life at sea in the attempt.[6] In Philadelphia, Rapp's disciples grew restless; some languishing penniless, having sold their Württemberg homes hurriedly for half their value. Several sold themselves and their children as indentured servants. A few might have starved had it not been for the charity of the German Society of Philadelphia and the merchant Godfrey Haga, who became a trusted financial adviser to the Harmony Society. Others scattered and formed smaller groups, settling both east and west of the Harmonists. One group went off with Dr. P. Friderich Conrad Haller, one of the two friends who had accompanied Rapp to America. They established the Blooming Grove community in Lycoming County, Pennsylvania, and remained friendly with Rapp. By contrast, Rapp's bitter rival David Gloss deigned to call him a fraudulent, wealth-hungry tyrant and servant of the devil. Gloss led his group to settle in Columbiana County, Ohio.[7]

This growing discontent among his followers forced the beleaguered Rapp, in October 1804, to purchase a site for the common settlement of those who still saw him as God's anointed prophet. In the name of "George Rapp and his Associates," he bought a tract of land at $2.50 an acre from a private owner twenty-six miles north of Pittsburgh in Beaver County, Pennsylvania.[8] Rapp was indebted to the works of the German theologian Johann Herder for the name of his first town, Harmony (*Harmonie*), and of his Harmonist movement. Herder, especially in his *Ideas on Philosophy and the History of Mankind,* made the case for an inevitable progress toward harmonizing all of nature, truth, intelligence, and reason. Rapp took this process to be God's preparation for Christ's Second Coming. So he linked his movement to the German theological concept of *harmonie* to indicate his disciples' central place in this millennial development.[9]

It was no surprise when George Rapp imposed a purely communal organizational structure upon his disciples at Harmony. Religious communalism was well-known. Numerous religious movements in their early stages had adopted community of goods for group security, solidarity, and survival. It had been used as a method of organizing by first-century Christians in Jerusalem, Roman Catholic monastic orders, and the Hutterites of eastern Europe and Russia. In Pennsylvania, communal living had been embraced in colonial days by the Moravians of Bethlehem and the Seventh Day Baptists of Ephrata. For decades, Amish communities in Pennsylvania had persevered with dedicated cooperation just short of requiring a common purse. Everyone knew about the success of the large communal farming settlements of the Shakers, led by English immigrant Ann Lee, in New York and New England, and later in Kentucky and Indiana.

The Harmonist preacher cajoled his faithful into communal sharing as an economic necessity. How else could his large congregation of such widely differing financial needs and resources be kept together? Pooling their wealth and labor seemed a reasonable solution. More importantly, Rapp stressed the scriptural imperative for their latter-day revival of the collective strength of community of goods "even in a more perfect degree."[10] He pointed out that Jesus and his apostles held a common purse, which set an example for the original Christians.[11] Of Peter's congregation in

Jerusalem, it was written, "And all that believed were together, and had all things common; And sold their possessions and goods, and parted them to all men, as every man had need" (Acts 2:44–45). and "the multitude of them that believed were of one heart and of one soul: neither said any of them that ought of the things which he possessed was his own; but they had all things common" (Acts 4:32). It was natural for the Harmonist leader to emphasize verses 34 and 35: "Neither was there any among them that lacked: for as many as were possessors of lands or houses sold them, and brought the prices of the things that were sold, and laid them down at the apostles' feet."[12] He undoubtedly also reminded his people how sudden death was the consequence for Ananias and his wife, Sapphira, when they pretended to give all to the congregation, lying to Peter, the church, and to God (Acts 5:1–11). Rapp attributed the abandoning of communalism by Jesus's first followers to persecution and the world's not being ready.[13] What he may not ever have understood was that by lifting their communal requirement, along with the Jewish rites of blood sacrifice and circumcision, early Christian leaders encouraged Christianity's expansion into the Gentile world. That the autocratic Father Rapp never embraced such flexibility became an Achilles' heel for his Harmonist movement.

Many left Harmony in 1805 refusing this new demand for complete, lifelong financial sharing, this pure communism with a small "c." Nevertheless, about five hundred loyal Rappite men and women signed the first of many communal agreements called Articles of Association dated February 15, 1805. These original articles made George Rapp the chief executive officer and, with revisions, became the legal basis for the Harmony Society until it was dissolved in 1905.[14] Signers agreed on behalf of themselves, their heirs, and their descendants to freely give all their property to "George Rapp and his Society in Harmony, Beaver County, Pennsylvania"—thus the name "Harmony Society." They pledged to obey the society's

regulations and superintendents and to request no compensation for themselves or their children if they should withdraw. George Rapp and his society promised that members and their families would receive instruction in school and church necessary for their earthly and eternal well-being. They guaranteed members all the necessities of life, in sickness and health, until the end of their days even if sometimes they could not work.

Although the articles were written as a legal foundation for the Harmony Society, when they were submitted to the Pennsylvania legislature for incorporation in 1807, they did not contain any provision for members to recoup the value of property they had contributed if they should choose to leave. Aware that several Harmonist seceders were already suing to reclaim their property, the legislature rejected the articles as unconstitutional in 1808.[15] Therefore, not out of Christian charity but because he was forced to do so by civil rights protections in state law, Rapp revised the 1805 articles to include Article Six, which stated that if members should choose to leave in an orderly manner the society was to refund the value of the property they had donated without interest.[16] He subsequently renewed the agreement with his disciples on February 15, 1816.[17] Nevertheless, when departures occurred, the strong-willed leader usually honored this part of the agreement grudgingly and often only after protracted lawsuits, three of which reached the Supreme Court of the United States.

Even with all these difficulties, Harmony, Pennsylvania, quickly became an efficiently symmetric and attractive town thanks to an impressive array of building tradesmen and the skills of George Rapp's son, John, as a surveyor. Its early log cabins and its later brick dwellings and large church eventually accommodated upwards of two thousand residents.[18] Fields and orchards yielded grains and fruits that soon fed them well. Mills and light manufacturing supplied many of their own needs and attracted a lucrative trade with neighbors. Harmonist whiskey, beer, and wine (which was kept in vaulted wine cellars in each of their three towns), as well as shoes, clothes, soap, candles, nails, and barrels, all found a ready market.

The German cultural heritage which the Harmonists brought in the marrow of their bones became abundantly evident first at Harmony, then New Harmony, and finally at Economy. Flower gardens flourished beside each house. A circuitous hedge labyrinth in each village challenged walkers to find a small structure in the middle whose rough-hewn exterior symbolized the difficulties of life and its beautiful interior the rewards of true harmony.[19] Music became the Rappites' crowning religious and cultural expression. Visitors never failed to testify to the centrality of music in Harmonist life—for individuals, choral groups, church services, bands, and orchestras.[20] As pietists, the Harmonists generally scorned religious icons, but a few visual motifs appeared throughout Harmonist history. These grew out of the mysticism Rapp first learned from reading the medieval German mystics Heinrich Suso and Johannes Tauler. They surfaced in sculpted lintels at Harmony—millennial roses, pure lilies reminiscent of Christ, and the Virgin Sophia as the spiritual wisdom Adam lost along with his rib and which Rapp's faithful tried to regain by their celibacy.[21]

At Harmony during a revival of pietistic perfectionism in 1807, celibacy became the paramount issue. To renew their commitment as Christ's return came ever nearer, the Harmonists vowed to purify themselves by sacrificing sexual pleasures and reproduction. Romelius Langenbacher, later known as R. L. Baker when he became head trustee of the society, remembered, "It was realized that the true imitation of Christ demanded more than natural man suspected or believed. This realization led . . . to a more serious conviction to lead a pure life. This had a strong effect on old and young and convinced us that we should live a life of self-denial and discipline, as is written: 'those who have wives as though they had none'" (I Corinthians 7:29).[22] To the Rappites these instructions

Sophia. Sculpted as an angel by Frederick Rapp, Bentel Building, Harmony, Pennsylvania.

Photo by Donald Pitzer.

from St. Paul for awaiting Christ's coming meant that even in marriage they should deny themselves the sexual privilege. Jesus had not married and Rapp's perfectionists determined to be among the 144,000 redeemed from the earth who would stand with the Lamb of God on Mount Zion as "those who did not defile themselves with women," as described in Revelation 14:1–4. Following the lead of mystic Jacob Boehme, Father Rapp taught sexual abstinence as a means to restore harmony with oneself and with God. He also insisted that celibacy liberated individuals for greater congeniality within the community. "Where sensual pleasures with their wants cease," he wrote, "there begins a more liberal, higher and better enjoyment, a friendly sociability of brotherly minds, all serving and loving one another reciprocally and growing together to one sociable crown."[23]

Without any formal agreement, after 1807, it was understood among Rapp's devotees that both marital and premarital sexual relations were unacceptable—a lower state of grace. Married couples continued to sleep together in private dwellings in each of their three towns with but few pregnancies—not a mean feat compared to celibates in the monastic orders, who were separated male and female into monasteries and convents; or to the Shakers, whose brothers and sisters slept on opposite sides of dormitory hallways which were sometimes dusted with flour to reveal violators' footprints. Since Rapp's faithful expected Christ's return any day, adding more children seemed unwarranted. Marriage was not condoned, but under pressure by young Harmonists in love, Rapp is known to have performed at least eighteen weddings, all but six before 1817.[24] On November 15, 1807, he performed the wedding ceremony for his son, John, and Johanna Diem. The couple gave the Rapps their only granddaughter in 1808. Most Harmonists already had offspring. Their children, orphans, and children of poor and indigent outsiders added youthful qualities to the aging Harmonist communities and filled their schools and apprenticeships.

For the Harmonists and their society, celibacy had sobering consequences. As Christ's coming failed to occur over the decades, those who had borne children before committing themselves to celibacy could look for their lineage to continue through descendants who left the group and continued to propagate. In 2008, descendants of these Harmonists held their first reunion at Old Economy Village, the Rappites' last hometown. But for others who never married or were childless, celibacy resulted in generational suicide, their lineages ending when they died. Thus the number of Harmonists dwindled due to lack of natural increase, and this became the primary factor for the demise of the Harmony Society by 1905.

However, while the Harmonists' numbers declined to extinction, their economic fortune grew from an original working capital at Harmony of a meager $23,000 into many millions in today's dollars. Much of this growth in the next thirty years was due to the unusual level of business acumen of George Rapp's adopted son, Frederick. Frederick Reichert, a Rappite convert from a village near Iptingen and a stonemason by trade, had been welcomed as a resident in Rapp's own home after 1798. Rapp entrusted him with the separatists' common fund for ministering to the poor of Württemberg. He used Frederick's exceptional organizational skills to manage the first migrations to America. Frederick apparently began using the last name Rapp to better handle business affairs as George's representative when he himself made the crossing and arrived in the United States in 1804.[25] At Harmony, Frederick became the principal business agent for the Harmony Society, a position he held until his death in 1834. In 1824, he was described as "a tall, rawboned, sallow complexioned, serious and plain German" who wore "a small crowned hat with a large brim over long brown hair."[26] One of the few Harmonists who spoke English well, Frederick undoubtedly carried on more functions for the society in the outside world than any other Harmonist and never betrayed the trust placed in him by George Rapp and his fellow communitarians.

International attention first came to the Harmony Society because of a travel guide to America, *Travels in the United States in the years 1806, 1807, and 1809, 1810, and 1811*, published in 1812 in Britain by the Scottish cotton industrialist and traveler John Melish. Melish visited Harmony for a week in 1811. His book, which was read widely in several editions and excerpts, celebrated the building and agricultural achievements wrought by communal effort in Harmony's six short years. Most important, Melish emphasized what he knew his European readers would understand as a breakthrough of worldwide significance. For the first time, a communitarian group had proven that manufacturing arising from the technology of the Industrial Revolution could be used as a community's basic source of income, permitting them to approach self-sufficiency. This was promising to reformers like Robert Owen, who began to see communalism as a possible peaceful method of creating social change. However, at the same time it was threatening for leaders of the industrialized nations, who had anxiously wondered if and when their colonies might challenge their mercantile monopolies. The industrial success of the Harmony Society issued an unmistakable warning. Rapp's communal industrialists soon prided themselves on their nearly complete freedom from foreign-made goods. They advocated high tariffs on imports to protect and stimulate domestic production, actively supporting what became known in national politics as "the American System."[27]

Their decade at Harmony, Pennsylvania, thus proved both momentous and disappointing to the Harmonists. Here they organized their communal society in 1805. Here they accepted the radical pietistic move into celibacy by 1807. Here they established their reputation for honest and effective business dealings. And here they brought the Harmony Society to international attention by demonstrating for the first time that a communal group could create a viable economic base from manufacturing, in addition to agriculture. Unfortunately, Harmony's location had fatal flaws. It was too far north to grow sufficient grapes for winemaking to become their principal source of income. Its 4,500 acres fell short of what was needed to provide for the thousands still expected to immigrate from Württemberg. Harmony also had the disadvantage of being on the unnavigable Connoquenessing Creek, which precluded the development of significant commerce. These crucial disadvantages became reasons to relocate after ten years of hard labor—such hard labor while daily longing for Christ's return that some of the weary Harmonists must have been tempted to believe the old Swabian saying "Work, work, work, and die." Even so, Father Rapp's charisma and ability to rally his disciples with relentless references to their divine mission as the Sunwoman

Father George Rapp, possibly walking to church carrying his Bible. Sketch by Prince Maximilian of Wied during his visit to Economy, Pennsylvania, 1832.

Joslyn Art Museum, Omaha, Nebraska.

Map of New Harmony drawn from memory by Wallrath Weingartner, 1832

Courtesy of the State Museum of Pennsylvania, Pennsylvania Historical and Museum Commission.

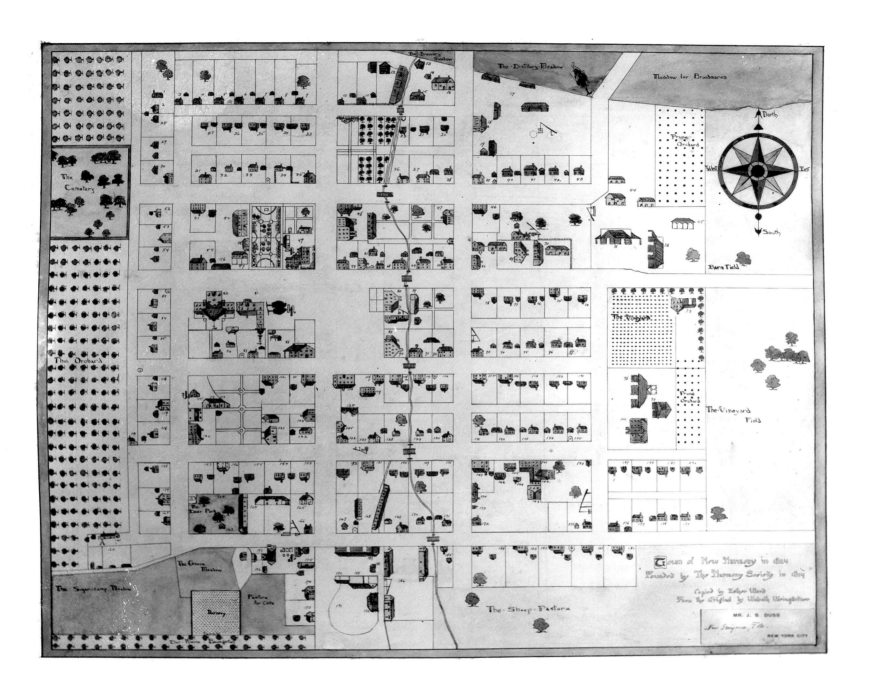

The Cemetery

The Orchard

The Sugar-camp Meadow

The Green Meadow

The Deer Park

Nursery

Pasture for Colts

The Drewery Meadow

The Distillery Meadow

Meadow for Broodmares

Prune Orchard

North

West   East

South

Barn Field

The Vineyard

Prune Orchard

The Vineyard Field

The Sheep Pasture

Town of New Harmony in 1824

Founded by The Harmony Society in 1814

Copied by Edwin Ward
From the Original by Wentworth Herington

MR. J. S. DUSS

New Smyrna, Fla.

NEW YORK CITY

of Revelation worked again. Before the Savior could return, they must move farther into the wilderness and build a *new* Harmony on enough land to accommodate the expected thousands of fellow Württemberg separatists, and in a milder climate where they hoped vineyards could thrive.

In April 1814, the fifty-six-year-old Father Rapp set out on horseback with two male companions for the frontier of the Indiana Territory, a journey reminiscent of his leaving Iptingen for America in 1803. As he passed through Kentucky, he wrote home that he was pleased that the achievements of the Harmony Society were already famous among people in the inns but that his spirit would not rest until he saw the Wabash. Rapp well knew that the navigable Wabash flowed to the Ohio, the Ohio to the Mississippi, and the Mississippi to New Orleans. Since he and Frederick had looked toward Louisiana for possible settlement while they were still in Germany, they fully understood that New Orleans had become a window to trade with the world. At New Harmony on the Wabash, their commercial dream would come true. From there, they would trade with twenty-two of the twenty four United States and at least nine foreign countries, including Canada, Cuba, Mexico, England, France, Germany, the Netherlands, Scotland, and Switzerland.[28]

Male and female hummingbirds, nest and eggs.
Watercolor by Wallrath Weingartner, 1829.

Courtesy of the State Museum of Pennsylvania, Pennsylvania Historical and Museum Commission.

HARMONIST NEW HARMONY, INDIANA (1814–1824)

On their mission from God, the three Harmonist horsemen persevered through thick forests and heavy underbrush, sometimes on old Indian trails, until Father Rapp found the perfect location for his new Harmony. On May 10, he wrote back to Frederick that "the place has all the advantages which one could wish." "The town will be located about ¼ mile from the river . . . on a plane as level as the floor of a room, perhaps a good quarter mile from the hill which lies suitable for a vineyard."[29] It was, in fact, one of the best

tracts of government land on the lower Wabash, fifteen miles from the mighty Ohio by land and sixty by river. At the land office in Vincennes, the Harmonist leader paid two dollars an acre, one-quarter down and the remainder over four years. After adding land purchased from pioneer owners who were often reluctant to sell, the Harmony Society eventually held twenty thousand acres, which were located on both sides of the river.[30]

This gave Rapp's saints an exclusive German enclave so secure in its cultural, religious, and economic monopolies as to cause its neighbors to suspect their motives and protest the prices at their

Red Owl. Watercolor by Wallrath Weingartner, 1829.

Courtesy of the State Museum of Pennsylvania, Pennsylvania Historical and Museum Commission.

store and mills, reminiscent of earlier concerns in Congress when it denied the Harmonist request for a secluded refuge in the West. Little wonder that the Harmonist prophet, having found his long-dreamed-of haven, should be the first person known to celebrate the Wabash River in verse. One can imagine his gazing out from its forested shores in 1814 and composing this refrain to comfort and inspire those who were to sing it on their arduous voyage from Harmony: "Wabash, Wabash, we'll see you soon" ("Wabash, Wabash, sehen wir bald").[31] Rapp must have felt the same emotion that later gripped Paul Dresser when he penned "On the Banks of the Wabash Far Away," which Hoosiers chose as the Indiana State Song.

During the first year of settlement, the old colony at Harmony, Pennsylvania, became the lifeline of supplies for the struggling new colony on the Wabash, much as present-day Hutterites help sustain

offspring "daughter colonies" in states of the U.S. Northwest and Canada during their initial years. Foodstuffs and, finally, almost all the movable property from Harmony, including cattle, were floated in some thirty flatboats and keelboats nearly a thousand miles to New Harmony along with a thousand Harmonists.[32] This Herculean feat was accomplished without accident, but thirteen members of the advance party succumbed to fever and had to be buried en route. Two hundred and thirty died of malaria, typhus, and other ailments before and after the swamps were drained.[33] All were buried in unmarked graves.

Overcoming such early challenges to their survival, these religiously motivated German peasants began to clear land. George Rapp was familiar with the modern, rectilinear town design that was in vogue in a few progressive cities from Württemberg to Pennsylvania.[34] His strong interest in this plan derived also from his admiration for the utopian communal Christian republic described and illustrated in Johann Valentin Andreae's *Christianopolis (Reipublicae Christianopolitanae Descriptio)*, which was published in Latin in 1619 and reprinted in a popular 1741 German edition that was read by Rapp. Andreae was a fellow Swabian, mystical seeker, and alchemist, whose visionary ideas, including the grid plan, attracted the Harmonist town builder. John Rapp had employed this efficient design for Harmony, and Frederick used it again as he drew the plan for Harmony, Indiana. Understandably, they began to call their town "new Harmony" (*neu Harmonie*), though some still make the error of thinking that Robert Owen renamed the town New Harmony when he bought it in 1825. On August 8, 1814, still considered the town's birthday, Frederick and a surveyor from Vincennes staked out ten wide streets that intersected at right angles and were centered on the town square.[35] Originally lined with shady and decorative Lombardy poplar trees, the streets still carry their descriptive names: West, Main, Brewery, and East going north to south, and North, Granary, Church,

New Harmony on the Wabash River. Watercolor by Karl Bodmer, 1833.

Original engraving in Prince Maximilian Alexander Philipp Zu Wied-Neuwied, Travels in the Interior of North America, *1832–1834, 2 vols. (London: Ackermann, 1843).*

Harmonist log dwelling, known as the Barrett Gate House. Built with prefabricated framing pieces marked with Roman numerals, c. 1814–1816.

Photo by Donald Pitzer.

Tavern, Steammill, and South running east to west.[36] Rectangular lots were laid out in uniform size, large enough for each family to have its own house and garden, its own pigs, chickens, and a barn that included an indoor outhouse. Each family's cow was kept in a central barn and was driven by the family home each morning and evening for milking. Soon the community's orchard was planted, its pastures were filled with cattle and prize Merino sheep, and two thousand acres were brought under cultivation.[37]

In 1832, Wallrath Weingartner, the most noted Rappite artist and mapmaker, drew from memory a map of New Harmony showing the physical appearance of its structures.[38] This sketch proved invaluable for creating the large-scale model of the historic village for the visitors' center, the Atheneum, which was designed

by Richard Meier and opened in 1979. Many of Weingartner's early Americana watercolor paintings of flowers and birds survive. His sketchbook, dated January 15, 1829, contains sixty-seven birds painstakingly copied from Alexander Wilson's *American Ornithology.*

Visitors to New Harmony during the Harmonist decade on the Wabash testified to the grandeur of the settlement, making its achievements ever more nationally and internationally famous. No fewer than twenty books written by foreign travelers in America described Rappite New Harmony.[39] After only five years, in 1819, Richard Flower of the nearby English community at Albion, Illinois, described the village as "that Wonder of the West."[40] Noted American economist and publisher Mathew Carey concluded in 1824 that "the settlement made more rapid advances in wealth and

Roman number marking on framing piece of a dwelling in George Rapp's hometown of Iptingen, Germany.

Photo by Donald Pitzer.

Harmonist frame dwelling, the Jacob Schnee House, 1906.

Courtesy of Special Collections, University of Southern Indiana.

prosperity, than any equal body of men in the world at any period of time, more in one year, than other parts of the United States ... have done in ten.[41] Karl J. R. Arndt, prominent Harmonist scholar, asserted that the per capita wealth of the Harmony Society by 1824 was ten times that of the average in the United States.[42]

The town rose in two phases that depended on the materials, equipment, and manpower available. Between 1814 and 1819, most structures were of poplar and oak logs chinked with wooden shims and clay grouting mixed with straw and river shells. (See color plates, pp. 94, and 179–80.) Each log dwelling had a stove used for heating and cooking, but not for baking since that was done in community ovens located in each block. With glass unavailable, the cabins initially had no windows. Walls were whitewashed and floors were scrubbed with sand, lye, and hot water to deter vermin.[43]

After 1819, with the construction of a saw mill and a brick kiln, frame and brick homes were built in front of the earlier log cabins.[44] Uniformity marked the new dwellings just as it had the humbler log ones, continuing the town's air of neatness and equality. Each type of structure had the same dimensions so Rappite builders could employ the quick and efficient German device of giving each framing piece a Roman numeral. (See color plates, pp. 138–39.) Such markings, like an early form of prefabrication, can still be seen on one of the earliest log cabins, now the Barrett Gate House, on the corner of North and Main Streets. For insulation and fire-proofing, each frame and brick home and several other community buildings had "Dutch biscuits," foot-long boards wrapped in straw and mud, secured in the floors, walls, and roofs. (See color plate, p. 118.) Each house had a single side entrance away from the dusty street. Each had a kitchen, a common room, and a stairway hall

View of Church Street from the south. George Rapp mansion with stone granary to the left. Pencil sketch attributed to David Dale Owen.

Courtesy of the New Harmony Working Men's Institute.

on the first floor and a stair hall and two bedrooms on the second. Each had plastered walls and ten windows located high enough for privacy.[45] (See color plates, pp. 89 and 140.)

The residence of the Harmony Society founder was more elaborately built, not an unusual practice among communal groups. "Mr. Rapp's house is a handsome brick building, by far the best in Indiana," observed Elias P. Fordham an Englishman who lived at Alton, Illinois.[46] It was a large, two-story mansion on the central square where Main and Church Streets intersect. A promenade like a captain's walk on the roof let Rapp survey his communal domain. From there he could also watch the night skies for comets, signs that Christ would come soon; while on a trip to Europe, Frederick reported some such harbingers back to him.[47] Amid these gracious surroundings, Father Rapp directed the affairs of the Harmony Society. He shared his spacious abode with Mrs. Rapp,

daughter Rosina, daughter-in-law Johanna, and granddaughter Gertrude, who grew up in the adoring eyes of her grandparents after her father died in a mill accident in 1812. She became the darling of the society as she developed her social graces to become the Harmonist hostess. At multicourse dinners for important visitors in the Rapp mansion, Gertrude often sang and displayed her talent on the pianoforte. She also painted in watercolors, created wax flowers, and set up an early petting zoo with her pet elk and other animals. Some of her writing was selected for the book of the Harmonists' best prose and poetry they published as *Fiery Coals* (*Feurige Kohlen*) in 1826. George, whose command of English never reached a comfortable level, usually spoke to outsiders through an interpreter, but Frederick and Gertrude became fluent in the language of their new homeland. She studied English in school and worked to perfect her speech in an extended visit with the Shakers at their West Union settlement, north of Vincennes. Later, at Economy, she won national recognition for her management of the Harmonists' award-winning silk production.[48]

By the early 1820s, four impressive three-story brick community houses had been constructed. These accommodated single members and families reduced by deaths from a plague of diseases. Referred to as Numbers 1, 2, 3, and 4 by the Harmonists, two of these heavy timber structures still survive for tours and public use. No. 2, with its adjoining brick kitchen, was located conveniently across Main Street from Rapp's mansion, where a large sundial hung. Later, it became the town clock on the south-facing wall of Community House No. 2, where it remained for most of the twentieth century. Now a replica can be seen in its place. (See color plate, p. 116.) On April 12, 1823, Number 2, by then also known as the Brother House (*Bruder Haus*), became the venue for one of the most pleasantly memorable days in Harmonist history, especially for relations between the generations. Father Rapp confided to his diary:

Gertrude Rapp's elk at New Harmony. Watercolor by Gertrude Rapp.

Courtesy of the State Museum of Pennsylvania,
Pennsylvania Historical and Museum Commission.

At noon we ate dinner with our entire family in Brother House number two. . . . I had a glass of wine served to all who belonged to house two. . . . In the evening around six, music began to play in the upper story of number 2 and all people gathered there uncalled, and I was very cheerful and happy for the oldest men and women sat in the hall to the right and left and there was a discussion about the beginning of the Harmonie. And young people sang several songs from the Harmony Songbook. Then we prayed. After that all the inhabitants of the house came and shook hands and promised not to break the bond of peace. And at 9:30 o'clock we parted.[49] (See color plate, p. 184.)

In addition to dwellings, New Harmony's 180 structures included mills, workshops, granaries, a general store, tavern-hotel, school, and two churches.[50] Rapp's town eventually contained six mills, including grain, oil, hemp, and saw mills. Most used water or animal power, but a grain mill featured one of the only steam engines on the frontier. As early as 1820, the Harmonists boasted of being all but self-sufficient. As strong advocates of protective tariffs, they especially hated competing with foreign imports. In their factories, seventy-five men, a dozen women, and thirty boys and girls produced fine woolen, cotton, and flannel cloth, leather goods, clothing, shoes, rope, and other necessities. These were given free to members at their store while outsiders were required to pay cash. Sometimes the Rappite brass band led men, women, and children joyfully to their labors in the grain fields, where they were known to harvest as much as a hundred acres in a day. The bountiful produce was stored in two granaries, one a massive, five-story, stone and brick structure.

The Rappites called their tavern the "tavern-house" (*Wirzhaus*) because it served the public as an inn with its own kitchen, stables, and wine cellar.[51] Here, travelers enjoyed the frontier luxury of neatly kept rooms, clean beds, and towels. William Faux, an English visitor, praised it as "the best and cleanest which I have seen in Indiana."[52] Elias Fordham reported: "The Tavern is conducted in the most orderly and cleanly manner that a tavern can

Harmonist Community House No. 2. White sundial is
visible on end wall. Photo, 1905. Don Blair Collection.

Courtesy of Special Collections, University of Southern Indiana.

be in America, where men spit *every where,* and, almost on *every thing.*"[53] Travelers and local neighbors alike enjoyed the fine quality Harmonist whiskey, beer, and wine. However, tavern patrons who became drunk and unruly were quickly thrown out, eliciting Fordham's comment that "the country people hate the Harmonists very much, because they permit no drunkenness in their taverns."[54]

Rapp's disciples themselves, having given up tobacco and sex after the 1807 revival, nevertheless indulged their German love of strong drink, especially the beer they produced after 1816 in Indiana's first commercial brewery.[55] On May 1, 1819, an advertisement in the Vincennes *Western Sun* proclaimed "F. Rapp, Will always have on hand, *and for sale,* THE FIRST QUALITY OF STRONG BEER, *by the Barrel,* at Harmony, Indiana." Soon the Harmony

Society sold the lucrative surplus from its brewery, distillery, and vineyards to hard-drinking frontiersmen in its own stores in Vincennes and in Albion and Shawneetown, Illinois, as well as through agents up and down the Ohio and Mississippi Rivers. Barrels of their coveted beer and whiskey sent to St. Louis and New Orleans often arrived lighter, the boatmen having taken their free nips.[56] The lobby of the New Harmony Inn now occupies the site of the Harmonist brewery northwest of the intersection of Brewery and North Streets. Nearby, visitors can still view the Rappites' brick hop house, which was used in the drying process so important in the production of their superior brews. (See color plate, p. 157.) A German visitor compared one variety favorably to "a real Bamberg beer." The Harmonist agent in Louisville reported: "Mr. Breeden, the most celebrated porter seller in this place says the strongest part of it would almost pass for porter and is the best beer he has ever seen in this country."[57] George Bentel, whose remodeled house remains just a block south of the brewery he managed, proudly directed the beer making in all three Harmonist towns. Without doubt, he would be pleased to know that in 2010 Hoosiers could once again taste his beer, or something very like it. Some thirty breweries of the Brewers of Indiana Guild, using archived copies of the very instruction books used by Bentel, reproduced his best beer, Indiana's first, as their 2010 Replicale.[58]

In the Harmony Society's second village, not only the rectilinear physical features but also the cultural dimensions of Andreae's ideal Christianopolis became more evident. Andreae would have been proud of the comprehensive educational program Rapp designed for children, teenagers, and adults in imitation of the one in Christianopolis. The Harmonist leader meticulously followed its formula—careful selection of teachers, free coeducational schooling from ages six to fourteen, and a broad curriculum complemented by vocational training in useful trades as well as the use of libraries, laboratories, museums, and printing presses as teaching tools. Rapp chose two of the society's cultural leaders, Christopher Mueller and Frederick Eckensberger, as principal teachers. Mueller, the headmaster at Harmony and New Harmony, was one of the two close friends Rapp brought with him to America in 1803. University educated, Mueller was the community's physician and director of music. When the society acquired a printing press in 1824, Mueller became the printer and printing instructor.[59] Eckensberger was both the innkeeper and a composer.[60] These men and others taught classes modeled after both utopian Christianopolis and the practical Lutheran vernacular free schools of Württemberg. Girls as well as boys met six days a week from 8:00 A M until noon. In 1819, between eighty and one hundred children aged six to twelve attended.[61] An English visitor that same year testified that "their school appears to be well conducted by a very respectable tutor who has a large number of scholars of different ages and of both sexes; all clean, neat and orderly."[62] In addition to Harmonist children such as Gertrude Rapp, students included orphans, indentured servants, and others assigned by the courts as wards of the Harmony Society.[63] By 1822, classes were conducted in the two-story schoolhouse on Tavern Street, which stood until 1913.

The Rappite school taught not only the "three Rs" ("reading, 'riting, and 'rithmetic") but also history, geography, drawing, vocal and instrumental music, and Latin, German, English, and French grammar. Classes were conducted in English on Monday through Wednesday and in German the last three school days of each week, a practice aimed at making the rising generation bilingual.[64] Indoctrination being integral to parochial education, Harmonist students studied from Luther's translation of the Bible and catechism but with Rapp's millennial and pietistic slant. The best writing, crafts, and artwork were chosen for display at church services on Sunday mornings. The curricular offerings and array of facilities for learning that Rapp put in place for an entire community from childhood through adulthood was unprecedented in the American West if not in most of the nation. The State of Indiana did not have a universal tax-supported public school system for another half century.[65] "Rappites" is still proudly emblazoned across the uniforms of New Harmony's athletic teams.

Apprenticeships after grammar school for the youth of New Harmony reflected the ongoing need for a skilled workforce to support the communal economy. It also demonstrated the fact that, for all his love of theology, philosophy, and literature, George Rapp was one of the most practical of men. Again and again, he had proven his own considerable knowledge and technical skills. He directed the construction of Harmonist towns with buildings whose plans he designed, farms whose soil types he recognized, and factories whose water-power sites he developed. Although he believed that "the proper education of Youth, is of the greatest importance to the prosperity of any plan, for the melioration of mankind," he also embraced Andreae's vocational training system, asserting, "That kind of learning, and those fashionable accomplishments, which are useless and only calculated for show, should be entirely abolished."[66] Therefore a seemingly endless variety of experienced farmers, vine dressers, orchard keepers, master craftsmen, and housewives of the Harmony Society taught their trades and talents to eager apprentices. Brewers and carpenters, millers and meat cutters taught their male charges. However, Rapp held to Andreae's plan by restricting girls' occupational instruction to gender-specific sewing, weaving, and spinning—one of the few limitations on women within a religious movement that granted women more equality than the outside world in most physical, intellectual, and political activities. Harmonist women not only received an equal academic education, they voted in community affairs, performed music in public, and controlled the sanctity of their own bodies in a patriarchal age—possibly not so much an issue within a voluntarily celibate community.[67] In total, the apprentice system ensured the ongoing truth of Rapp's claim that "here wealth is possessed in abundance, and all cares for subsistence, are removed and forgotten."[68]

Adults of both sexes enjoyed a wide variety of opportunities for intellectual and cultural enrichment within their own frontier community. They were offered evening classes in English and arithmetic. They were encouraged to read the wide assortment of newspapers and books available at their store. They had access to the society's library, one of the most extensive in the western states. Its more than 350 volumes ranged beyond theology and philosophy to science, medicine, and literature.[69] Father Rapp urged the entire New Harmony community to enter a prose and poetry competition with the best submissions to be printed on their own press. The resulting volume, *Fiery Coals* (*Feurige Kohlen*), offers a rare look into the emotional depths of the pious hearts and minds of ordinary Harmonists. Adults as well as young people were invited into choral and instrumental music groups, the orchestra, and the town's brass band. Their band, possibly Indiana's first, entertained the community on Saturday nights from the balcony at the base of the steeple atop the brick church. The sound of its French horns awakened everyone each workday morning. Hundreds of Rappites made their own handwritten hymnals embellished with their watercolor artwork.[70] A few, like Mueller and Eckensberger, composed music, especially hymns. These and other Harmonist favorites were printed on their own press in 1824 as A *Small Collection of Harmonist Songs* (*Eine kleine Sammlung Harmonischer Lieder*). It was likely the first songbook published in Indiana.[71] During the Harmony Society's history, the quantity of both religious and secular music that the Harmonists knew, performed, and appreciated was enormous. They even commissioned outside composers like William C. Peters, who discovered Stephen Foster. This alone ranks them among the communal Moravians, Shakers, and Seventh Day Baptists of the Ephrata Cloister, whose music they also admired and emulated.[72]

While still in the wilds of New Harmony, Christopher Mueller began collecting specimens for a natural history museum, which was an important feature of Christianopolis. This taxidermy collection grew into the extensive Rappite wildlife museum in the Feast Hall at Economy, which became a popular public educational attraction. Although many of the original specimens were dispersed when the society was dissolved in 1905, this museum was refurbished and replenished in the 1990s as the oldest natural history museum in America still in its original building.

Gardening became a learning experience in each family's yard and led to important innovations. Christopher Mueller also began a botanical garden to experiment with medicinal plants. His breakthroughs became so important that other herbalists, including the nationally known Constantine Rafinesque, made visits to examine his garden and discuss the latest developments in herbal cures.[73] Mueller's work set a precedent in the Indiana wilderness a half century before Eli Lilly began producing medicines based first on herbs then on chemical synthesis that made Indianapolis a pharmaceutical capital. In his spacious formal garden and unique mobile greenhouse Father Rapp indulged his experimental urge, an urge that later became his troublesome obsession with alchemy. To expose or protect his fragile varieties of strawberries, orange trees, flowers, and other plants, his greenhouse could slide off or over them depending on the weather.[74]

Everyone found the five-acre pleasure garden on the south edge of town an educational and recreational treat. With its medicinal herbs, flowering shrubs, dwarf fruit trees, and challenging labyrinth, it was a unique German attraction on the American frontier. The labyrinth was constructed of various types of vines and shrubs laid out in concentric circles some 140 feet in diameter. First-timers were puzzled not just by its paths but by the mysterious little building the successful ones reached in the middle. For Harmonists the search represented the difficulty of finding the harmonious meaning of life, which was symbolized by the shrine in the center with its rough-hewn exterior but beautifully furnished and colorfully painted interior.[75] Miner Kellogg, who explored the labyrinth as a lad during Owen community days, later recalled his shocking experience with its unexpected surprises:

> Its lines were formed of vines grown upon light fences and about four feet high, converging as they reached the centre. Here the visitor came upon a circular hut made of the ends of rough logs cut to a point externally leaving one window—& a blind door which had to be sought out—& only found by pushing at the walls. I remember well my first visit to this hut, after a long & tedious run back and forth through the labyrinth. On seeking for the door a large snake took a look at me from between the logs, laughing at me with its long red tongue. I got back out of the labyrinth much sooner and easier than I found my way in.[76]

This Harmonist landmark disappeared over the years. Then, in 1939, it was replanted on an adjacent site. Visitors today still wander its paths to find the peace and harmony within its central temple, which was rebuilt in 1941. (See color plates, pp. 128–30.) The historic Harmonist labyrinth has inspired such local interest that in recent years two others have been constructed: one in New Harmony and the other at the University of Southern Indiana in Evansville, both patterned after the famous labyrinth in Chartres Cathedral. (See color plate, p. 92.)

All these Harmonist educational and leisure activities were part of a life of intellectual, social, and religious fulfillment. Although they shunned sex, drunkenness, and tobacco, the Rappites were not ascetics like some Catholic monastic orders or the Seventh Day Baptists of Ephrata. Celibate husbands and wives slept together. Families lived together. Although all led active, industrious lives, they were not intentionally overworked, though Rapp did not tolerate what he called "sluggards." Many hands and seasonal jobs lightened the labor. In addition to July Fourth, six holidays punctuated their calendar—Christmas, Easter, Pente-

cost, Harmoniefest (commemorating February 15, the date when the original Articles of Association were signed in 1805), Erntefest (harvest festival in early August, now reflected in New Harmony's annual Kunstfest; see color plates 3 and 62), and Liebesmahl ("love feast" to mark the Lord's Supper in late October).[77] Visitors testified that the Rappites ate abundantly, and they were known to stage huge public picnics to placate their often disgruntled neighbors. If Harmonist clothing appeared simple and somber to outsiders, resembling that of present-day Amish and Hutterites, it was practical, comfortable, and uniform in the tradition of German peasants. The Rappites produced cloth for sale in reds, greens, and yellows but modestly chose the dark colors for themselves. In his diary, Owenite Donald Macdonald described the men as having long hair and dressing in plain brown or blue frock coats or surtouts, trousers, and shoes. The women, he noted, wore cloth gowns with checkered neckerchiefs and aprons and white caps.[78] William Faux, the English traveler, saw the people as shabby, "just as working folk in general." "None are genteel," he said. "The women are intentionally disfigured and made as ugly as it is possible for art to make them, having their hair combed straight up behind and before, so that the temples are bared, and a little skullcap, or black crape bandage, across the crown, and tied under the chin."[79]

The two New Harmony churches symbolized the millennial faith that compelled Rapp's Sunwoman to flee into the backwoods of Indiana. Erecting the first church, a three-story frame building, became an early priority. This was the first place in New Harmony the entire membership could gather at one time. Finished in 1816, this impressive white edifice with its tall spire faced the morning sun and dominated the square across Church Street from George Rapp's mansion. A visitor in 1819 wrote that this sanctuary, "with its steeple, clock, and bell, is of course the most conspicuous building: it has three floors; but the lower one only is used for public worship."[80] Frederick made the large bell's dual purpose very clear in his special order to an English foundry. The Harmony Society, he wrote, "possesses 25,000 Acres of Land in one Tract and the Bell is chiefly intended to notify particular Hours of the Day to the Members who may be occupied in different, and at times distant parts of the settlement. The sound should therefore not only be solemn, but loud."[81] It was said that this bell could be heard seven miles outside the village.

Accounts of services and other meetings on Sundays and weekdays were reported by visitors allowed to attend. Elias Fordham, who had become a closer friend than all but a few outsiders, noted in his *Personal Narrative* in 1818: "The men sit at one end of the church and the women at the other; and Mr. Rapp sits while he preaches in a chair placed on a stage, about one yard high, with a table before him. When I heard him one week day evening, he wore a linsey wool coat and a blue worsted night cap. In praying the Harmonists do not rise up or kneel down, but bend their bodies forward, almost to their knees. Their singing is very good."[82] Morris Birkbeck, interested observer and co-founder of the English settlement at Albion, Illinois, noted one Sunday evening that "soon the entire body of people, which is about seven hundred, poured out of the church, and exhibited so much health and peace and neatness in their persons, that we could not but exclaim, surely the institutions that produced so much happiness must have more of good than evil in them."[83]

Unfortunately, this frame church became so unbearably hot during the humid southern Indiana summers that Father Rapp had to design a new one with thick, insulating brick walls.[84] Some said its cruciform design came to him in a dream, although its floor plan, in the shape of a Greek cross, was well-known at the time. Begun in 1822 and not quite finished when Robert Owen came to inspect the town for purchase in December 1824, the second church, called the Community House (*Gemeinde Haus*),

Harmonist white frame church. 1821 sketch by Ablard Welby printed in his *A Visit to North America and the English Settlements in Illinois,* 1821.

Harmonist brick cruciform church with the Door of Promise entrance and to its left the frame church after losing its steeple. Sketch attributed to David Dale Owen, 1830. Source unknown.

rose just west of the first. In anticipation of new arrivals from Germany, its 120-foot-long arms and 80-square-foot central sanctuary could seat many more than the current membership. Harmonist craftsmen lavished their skills on this spacious structure. Before they had it quite finished, the English travel writer William Hebert observed: "These people exhibit considerable taste as well as boldness of design. . . . They are erecting a noble church, the roof of which is supported in the interior by a great number of stately columns, which have been turned from trees of their own forests. The kinds of wood made use of for this purpose are . . . black walnut, cherry, and sassafras. Nothing I think can exceed the grandeur of the joinery, and the masonry and brick-work seem to be of the first order." Almost euphoric, Hebert continued enthusiastically, "I could scarcely imagine myself to be in the woods of Indiana, on the borders of the Wabash, while pacing the long resounding aisles, and surveying the stately colonnades of this church. Here too the Englishman is once more gratified with the sound of a church bell . . . after a period of estrangement from it . . . infinitely more soothing than could [be] the most delicate strains of music."[85]

William Faux, who suspected Rapp was a tyrannical high priest ruling over his superstitious German slaves, described the scene as the Harmonists rushed to their ten o'clock Sunday service—which he was not allowed to attend:

> At the moment the bells began chiming, one and all from every quarter, hurry into their fine church like frightened doves to their windows; the street leading to the temple seems filled in a minute, and in less than ten minutes, all this large congregation, 1,000 men, women, and children, all who can walk or ride, are in the church, the males entering in at the side, the females at the tower, and separately seated. Then enters the old High Priest, Mr. Rapp . . . straight and active as his adopted son, Frederick, who walks behind him. The old man's wife and daughters [possibly daughter Rosina and daughter-in-law Johanna] enter with the crowd from his fine house, which looks as if the people who built it for him, thought nothing too good for him.[86]

Neither of the churches survived the nineteenth century. In 1874, Jonathan Lenz, whose father David's house in New Harmony is part of a guided tour (see color plates, pp. 89–90), was sent from Pennsylvania by the Harmony Society to purchase the brick, cruciform church and oversee its demolition. The bricks were used to build a wall around the Harmonist burial ground—a cemetery originally in the orchard where no gravesites were marked because all were equal in death and soon to be resurrected in Christ's kingdom.[87] On August 23, 1980, representatives from the German province of Württemberg placed four bricks from George Rapp's hometown of Iptingen in this wall during a twinning ceremony.

The principal function of these churches was to keep the imminent second coming of Christ foremost in the consciousness of

Harmonist Cemetery. Deceased members buried in the orchard in unmarked graves. Wall built of bricks from their church in 1874. Don Blair Collection.

Courtesy of Special Collections, University of Southern Indiana.

each Harmonist. Father Rapp's sermons and writings constantly stirred the utopian millennial fervor. He stressed Jesus's promise: "If I go and prepare a place for you, I will come again, and receive you unto myself; that where I am, there you may be also" (John 14:3). "And Jesus said, I am: and ye shall see the Son of man sitting on the right hand of power, and coming in the clouds of heaven" (Mark 14:62). "Blessed are those servants, whom the lord when he comes shall find watching." (Luke 12:37). Millennialism defined their mission and motivated their lives. Their singing rang from the rafters in anticipation of the joyous event. Frederick Rapp designed a reminder on the front entrance to the brick church, which became known as the Door of Promise. This door is seen today in replica at its original location, facing north onto Church Street. (See color plates, pp. 161 and 165.) The stone lintel features an elliptical wreath containing the golden rose symbol for the mil-

lennium and its biblical reference in Micah 4:8. Only in Luther's translation of the Bible, the one read by the Rappites, does the golden rose appear in this verse, in reference to the New Jerusalem of the returning Lord: "And you, Tower of Eden, stronghold of the daughter of Zion, your Golden Rose shall come, the former dominion, the kingdom of the daughter of Jerusalem." European Christians in Luther's time understood the allusion. Popes gave a golden rose to kings in recognition of their work on behalf of God's kingdom. Therefore, Jerusalem would receive the highest possible award, a golden rose, as Christ made it the governmental center of his earthly kingdom for a millennium or more. *Golden Rose (Güldene Rose)* by Christoph Schutz was then a favorite millennial volume of German separatists.[88] Few Americans understood the potent symbolism, even though the Harmonists placed the golden rose as a trademark on their coveted products.

In New Harmony, however, the spirit of the Harmony Society's millennial golden rose lives on in the Roofless Church designed by Philip Johnson. Within its walls, a fifty-foot-tall representation of an inverted rosebud casts the shadow of a fully opened rose and overarches a sculpture by Jacques Lipchitz, *The Descent of the Holy Spirit.* Dedicated in 1960 and rededicated in 2010, the green grass of this interdenominational church is open to the sky to signify the universal quality of all faith. The Roofless Church is a venue for weddings, memorial services in celebration of life, and other sacred occasions. (See color plates, pp. 103–104, and 181.)

Rapp became so convinced that Christ would soon return that he took immediate measures to prepare. He had the congregation begin a "church fund" in gold and silver coins. This cash reserve in specie, known later as the "Jerusalem fund," was to guard the Harmony Society against the uncertainties of paper money in the last days and to bankroll the trip of a Harmonist delegation to the Holy Land to greet the returning Lord. This cash fund eventually grew to a half million dollars. After Rapp's death in 1847, it was

Millennial Door of Promise from the Harmonist brick church as used later in the New Harmony School. Photo, 1900. Don Blair Collection.

Courtesy of Special Collections, University of Southern Indiana.

Detail of the Door of Promise pediment on the entrance to the Harmonist brick church with the millennial golden rose and biblical reference to Micah 4:8 in Martin Luther's translation. Bas-relief carving attributed to Frederick Rapp.

Photo by Donald Pitzer.

discovered in a vault under his first-floor bedroom in his third town of Economy, Pennsylvania.

The persuasive Harmonist preacher emphasized current events that he thought were pointing ever more clearly to the ful- fillment of millennial prophecy. He scoured German and English newspapers, questioned travelers, and corresponded with friends in Europe and America to uncover evidence of the wars and ru- mors of wars, famines, pestilences, earthquakes, and signs in the heavens—like the comet sightings reported by Frederick during his business trip back to Württemberg—that indicated the im- minence of Christ's return (Matthew 24:6, Mark 13:7, Luke 21:9). For him Napoleon's escape from Elba, the Congress of Vienna, the formation of the Holy Alliance, fighting between France and Spain in 1823, and events in Italy and China fulfilled prophecies from the books of Daniel and Revelation.[89]

To summarize how historical trends demonstrated the pro- gression which he optimistically thought must precede and prepare the way for Christ's coming kingdom, the Harmonist prophet wrote a book. Later theologians labeled this interpretation "post-millennialism" as opposed to "pre-millennialism," which more pessimistically holds that world conditions will get worse and worse until Christ comes to effect reform.[90] Rapp titled his book *Thoughts on the Destiny of Man, particularly with reference to the present times (Gedanken über die Bestimung des Menschen, besonders in Hinsicht der gegenwärtigen Zeit)*. Printed on the Harmonist press in 1824 in both German and English, this volume of nearly one hundred pages is considered the first work on religious philosophy published in Indiana. However, neither the German version, which Rapp was still revising as late as 1831, or the English translation, which he disliked, was ever circulated.[91]

In his *Thoughts,* the Rappite leader drew heavily on his favorite German religious philosopher Johann Herder's *Ideas on a Philosophy of the History of Mankind (Ideen zur Philosophie der Geschichte der Menschheit)* and his *Letters for the Advancement of Humanitarianism (Briefe zur Beförderung der Humanität)*. Rapp made the title of his *Thoughts* parallel to that of Herder's *Ideas,* used his own utopian *Harmonie* as a synonym for Herder's ideal *Humanität,* and sometimes copied sections from Herder verbatim without giving him credit.[92] Rapp's book attempts to show that, beginning with the Enlightenment, advances in rational thought, human rights, republican forms of government, and all fields of knowledge were advancing the world toward the kingdom of God, which would be established in the nineteenth century. "It is our exalted period alone," he exclaims, "that can take such a high flight, and disseminate the blessings of the golden age."[93] He offers his own Harmony Society as proof that, despite all the evil still in the world, a "better race of man" has emerged as part of God's plan and has created a communal model of this "*heaven upon earth—A true HARMONY*" soon to be realized worldwide.[94] In one of the classic statements

in all of utopian literature, Rapp declares that his New Harmony has already become such a heavenly place:

> where those who occupy its peaceful dwellings, are so closely united by the endearing ties of friendship, confidence, and love, that one heart beats in all, and their common industry provides for all. Here, the members kindly assist each other, in difficulty & danger, and share with each other, the enjoyments, and the misfortunes of life; one lives in the breast of another, and forgets himself; all their undertakings are influenced by a social spirit, glowing with noble energy, and generous feeling, and pressing forward to the haven of their mutual prosperity. Noble Asylum! Where brethren live together in unity and love, & form upon Earth, a Kingdom of God.[95]

Despite Father Rapp's writings, sermons, and prophecies and New Harmony's churches and original music, their neighbors understood little of the deeper millennial meanings and motivations of the Harmony Society. This was true internationally as well. As travelers' journals were published and Harmonist goods were sold far and wide, the society became world-famous during its New Harmony decade. Unlike most other religious and communal groups, the Rappites did not actively proselytize once in America. Nevertheless, inquiries flooded the desks of George and Frederick from across the United States and Europe—letters of application for membership and questions about the secret of the Harmonists' economic success, their religious beliefs, and how to create similar communities. Robert Owen, the wealthy cotton manufacturer of New Lanark, Scotland, who would buy New Harmony and found the first communal experiment of his secular reform movement in 1825, wrote to ask about the Harmonists' secrets of success in 1820. Owen sent them his publications about reforming society and requested theirs. Such frequent requests for information and pamphlets about the organization, nature, and purposes of the society resulted in the purchase of the Rappite printing press on which Father Rapp's *Thoughts on the Destiny of Man* was printed. Ultimately, however, the press was only used for printing items for circulation within the community, such as the Harmonist hymnbook, so it never fulfilled the need to distribute information to the general public. Misconceptions and rumors lived on, and the golden rose trademark continued to convey little more than the high quality of Harmonist goods. Most outsiders knew only that this strange and industrious band of communal German Americans used a calculated balance of agriculture, manufacturing, and commerce to create a financial empire and employed their numbers and unity to wield political power.[96]

Professor Karl J. R. Arndt, the most prolific writer on the Harmony Society, concluded: "No politician who aspired to national, statewide, or county office considered it wise to run for office without first considering the Harmony Society."[97] This is not an exaggeration. The votes, advice, and assistance of the Rappite community influenced all three levels of government. After Posey County was created out of Gibson and Warrick Counties in 1814, Harmonists made up by far the majority of the citizens of this new county. When the Rappites' ballots were stolen or destroyed in one county election, Rapp had his voting bloc abstain in the next. The winner of that contest, who apparently had not expected their support, wrote to thank them for not voting.[98] Father Rapp wanted the benefits of the county seat, including its post office, *near* but not *in* his exclusive village. In 1817, by offering to build a courthouse in Springfield, just five miles away, he succeeded. Not until February 1825, just as the Harmonists were completing their move back to Pennsylvania, did the legislature move the courthouse to Mount Vernon. Alexander Devin, a delegate to the Indiana constitutional convention, warned George Rapp that if he used the overwhelming majority of his Harmony Society men to determine every political decision in Posey County the members of his community would incur the wrath of their neighbors and their safety and civil liberties might be jeopardized.[99] This fate later befell the communal Mormons in Missouri and Illinois where their leader, Joseph Smith, and others were killed.

Thomas Posey, last governor of the Indiana Territory, after whom Posey County was named, considered the Harmonist vote so important that while the 1816 Indiana constitutional convention was still in session he wrote Frederick a letter communicating his wish to be considered a candidate for governor of the new state.[100] When the Democratic-Republican Jonathan Jennings defeated him to become Indiana's first governor, it became apparent that the Harmony Society did not deliver the Posey County vote to Posey.

The Rappites achieved their antislavery and pacifistic goals at the constitutional convention in Corydon, to which Frederick Rapp was a delegate. Although Frederick at first voted not to apply for statehood, Harmonists preferring the fewer taxes and restrictions of territorial status, he served on important committees and got Harmonist objectives written into Indiana's first constitution. He joined heartily in the strong stand against slavery taken by Democratic-Republican delegates, which was written into the document. Consistent with their antislavery position, the Harmony Society managed to free several slaves through an indenture process at New Harmony.[101] Article VII of the new constitution provided that conscientious objectors could avoid military service by paying a fine. Pennsylvania already had a similar provision. However, during the War of 1812, the Harmony Society had so little cash it could not pay the fine for all its men. This matter became so contentious it was one reason the Harmonists moved west.[102] In Indiana, such military exemption was agreeable to the government since it provided a welcome, steady source of revenue for the new state treasury. But, as in Pennsylvania, it aroused jealousy, even hatred, among the Rappites' neighbors. The Harmony Society now had not only the money to free all its adult males from the risks of bearing arms, but also the right to deny the local militia needed recruits.[103] Whether in Württemberg, Pennsylvania, or Indiana, their refusal to become soldiers was perfectly logical to Rapp's emulators of Christ. They never practiced pacifism in the sense of protesting war itself, however. Using Jacob Boehme and the book of Revelation, they gave their own private religious interpretation to pacifism as to all things.[104] Opposing war would be futile because sinful man after Adam's fall would always engage in warfare just as he would always yield to his physical desire to have sex. Wars and procreation were inevitable. Thus, the Harmonists did not seem to mind if others participated in these brutal and beastly affairs, but they had been divinely chosen and perfected, making them unfit for such carnality.

In 1820, the Indiana legislature showed its respect for Frederick's expertise in drafting and town planning by putting him on the commission that chose the permanent site for the capital of Indiana. He drew and signed a map of the projected town of Indianapolis that was patterned after Washington, D.C., with which he was familiar. His drawing seems to have influenced the final design, which he also may have helped survey.[105] National legislators also noticed the political and economic importance of Harmonist New Harmony, keeping the Rapps informed and soliciting their counsel. Their congressman friend William Hendricks, later the third governor of Indiana, wrote them in February 1819 to bring them up-to-date on national affairs.[106]

No one knows exactly when or why Father Rapp decided to forsake his New Harmony utopia and lead his disciples back to Pennsylvania to build a third town. But everyone knew that by 1823 problems had arisen that must have made him conclude that conditions on the frontier were no longer tenable. His dream of much-expanded wine production was defeated by the Indiana climate. Malaria continued to stalk his community. And he never made lasting peace with his neighbors.[107] From the beginning many frontiersmen were suspicious, resentful, and sometimes violent toward Rapp's German settlement. Nowhere else in America had settlers seen a thousand disciples of a single prophet so ethnically, religiously, and socially different descend upon their region and establish such a political and economic monopoly. In the earliest days, men whom he hired to help clear the land conspired to charge exorbitant wages and threatened his life when he protested.[108] Possibly for his own protection, the Harmonist leader made his daily rounds to inspect his mills, fields, and factories dressed "as the meanest laborer," in the words of Elias Fordham. This could have made him virtually incognito since as Fordham further noted, "They all dress alike."[109]

All of New Harmony's neighbors understood the benefits its mills, factories, and stores brought to the settlers. But this did not lessen their dislike of the Harmonists' regional economic dominance which let them demand cash payment and charge more than the backcountry market could reasonably bear. In 1818, twenty-one Posey County men petitioned the Indiana General Assembly to declare the indispensable New Harmony grain mill public property.[110] Before the legislature acted to give the men some price relief, neighbors who were outraged at the grinding fees and store prices attacked several Harmonists and rioted for two hours in the streets of New Harmony on January 20 and 21, 1820.[111] Nine frontiersmen were arrested, and Frederick Rapp and tavern keeper Frederick Eckensberger were accused by outsiders of taking part in the fisticuffs.

If outsiders were surprised when these pacifistic Harmonists did not turn the other cheek, they also must have wondered why the Rappites bought a cannon and built a granary that could be used as a fort. Evidence suggests the cannon was fired only twice—once to celebrate the arrival of the first steamboat in 1823 and once to mark the departure of Father Rapp with the first boatload going back to Pennsylvania in 1824. On the first occasion, the men were so inept they overloaded the cannon and injured several bystanders, including a man who suffered a wound to his head and a boy who lost his foot.[112] By 1819, the Harmonists completed a second granary. With foot-thick stone and brick walls and ventilation slits that could be used as gun portals, this five-story structure gave the public impression that it was intended to double as a fort capable of sheltering all the hundreds of Rapp's disciples from attack. The Harmonists called it the stone granary (*Stein Fruchthaus*) and its street Granary Street (*Fruchthaus Strasse*).[113]

However, from the 1820s until it was attractively restored for public occasions in 1999, others spoke and wrote of it as "the fort." When James Miles Wattles, a student in the Owen community, made one of the first photographs in America in 1828, it was of what he called "the old fort."[114] When New Harmony historian George B. Lockwood published a photograph of the granary in 1905, he used the caption "The Old Fort as Built."[115] Was it a granary or a fort? The question, which has been debated for decades in New Harmony, has a simple answer. Fortified granaries (*Wehrscheuer*) were common structures in villages throughout Württemberg. Located right in town or on a nearby hill, they usually had a well inside and provided quick, effective refuge from periodic invaders, especially where there were no town walls, castles, or moats.[116] George Rapp grew up familiar with the small fortified granary in Iptingen. Given the security issues confronting New Harmony, he obviously drew on his knowledge of this and other such structures in Germany to create a facility that could both store grain and offer safety. He knew the protective potential of placing this granary conveniently in the middle of town only a half block from

Rappite stone granary, for years called "the Old Fort." Photo, 1906. Don Blair Collection. *Courtesy of Special Collections, University of Southern Indiana.*

his mansion instead of near the grain fields. During the excavation for the granary's 1999 adaptive reconstruction, an internal well was discovered that could have sustained those inside, as well as a bricked-in cubbyhole beneath the ground floor that could have served as a vault for the Harmonist bank. The door, which could be easily blocked if its huge wooden crossbar was lowered, locked on the inside with a nine-inch-long key that is now on display in the nearby Workingmen's Institute.[117] Fortunately, no threat from neighbors or the few Native Americans then south of Vincennes became so severe that Rapp's community needed such imposing physical protection. Perhaps the peace-loving Harmonists' cannon and fortified granary served them most effectively as their own passive defensive threats.

The deep economic depression that followed the War of 1812 undoubtedly carried the greatest weight in Father Rapp's decision to move his people back east to an area near Pittsburgh where German culture was commonly known and accepted, where financial conditions were more stable, and where markets were closer. The Indiana backcountry had been hit particularly hard by unstable currency and bank failures. That the Harmony Society maintained its financial success was a public testimony to its communal economy and the integrity of its business leaders. Nearly everyone who had dealings with the Harmony Society grew to realize that they could trust the honest dealings of Frederick Rapp and Johannes Langenbacher, who had been known as John L. Baker ever since he directed the advance party to New Harmony. To protect their own commercial transactions, the Rappites founded the Farmers Bank of Harmony with Frederick as president. Becoming a banking center in its own right, New Harmony did all in its power to help organize a sound banking system for the new state of Indiana but with discouraging results. Corruption and politics brought down other private "wildcat" banks, and even though Frederick was appointed a director of the state bank at Vincennes in 1821, previous mismanagement already had assured its failure. A little-known Harmonist legacy is that they directly contributed to the economic survival of the state. When its first governor, Jonathan Jennings, asked for a personal loan of $1,000, the Harmonist bank refused even at 10 percent interest; but when the state treasurer asked for a $5,000 loan to keep the state solvent in 1823, the bank stepped up to save the day at the usual 6 percent.[118] The fact that his Harmony Society alone in all of Indiana had the resources to sustain the financial underpinnings of the state confirmed Rapp in his conclusion: It was time to retreat from the economic jeopardy that surrounded his twenty-thousand-acre estate in the West.

Such a move also held promise for solving severe problems facing Rapp's millennial religious movement. If the thousands of disciples he expected from Germany had arrived, his Harmonists might have filled the new state of Indiana as the Mormons later filled Utah. But gradually it had dawned on the Harmonist prophet that he would not fill his German settlement on the Wabash. Two untimely developments robbed him of this opportunity. First, Württemberg authorities had become more tolerant of its separatists, making emigration less attractive. Second, in a nasty twist of prophetic fate, Johann Heinrich Jung-Stilling, the radical pietist who had popularized the Sunwoman prophecy in Germany, switched his scriptural interpretation of the wilderness to which she was to flee: by 1812, it was Russia, not America. Thousands who Rapp thought would join his Harmony Society in Indiana stayed in Württemberg. Others accepted free land in the Caucasus offered by Czar Alexander I, who had been convinced by Jung-Stilling that he was divinely anointed to create the Holy Alliance and shelter the Sunwoman.[119]

In addition to this stagnation in membership, Father Rapp faced dissent that threatened his authority and the unity of his New Harmony congregation. Committed young people who wanted to marry while remaining in the society induced Father Rapp to perform at least seven weddings.[120] Some revolted against the celibacy which had become so widely known that Lord Byron playfully challenged it in Canto XV of his *Don Juan*:

> When Rapp the Harmonist embargo'd marriage
> In his harmonious settlement—(which flourishes
> Strangely enough as yet without miscarriage,
> Because it breeds no more mouths than it nourishes,
> Without those sad expenses which disparage
> What Nature naturally most encourages)—
> Why call'd he "Harmony" a state sans wedlock?
> Now here I have got the preacher at a dead lock.
>
> Because he either meant to sneer at Harmony
> Or marriage, by divorcing them thus oddly.
> But whether reverend Rapp learn'd this in Germany

Or no, tis said his sect is rich and godly,
Pious and pure, beyond what I can term any
Of our, although they propagate more broadly.
My objection's to his title, not his ritual,
Although I wonder how it grew habitual.[121]

In 1818, as the rising generation became eager to know what their parents had given over to the society and what they might inherit, Rapp took the irreversible step of burning the account book.[122] His increasingly dictatorial excesses, including censorship of members' mail, caused some to choose the emotionally painful and financially precarious path of secession.[123] Despite the dangers of the frontier, forty-three left during the New Harmony decade. Frederika Vaihinger was the only woman known to risk leaving alone.[124]

In addition to economic jeopardy, membership stagnation, and youthful dissension, the community faced boredom once their building tradesmen completed New Harmony but Christ still had not come. So, once again, Father Rapp found a millennial justification for his Harmony Society to move like the Sunwoman of prophecy. In sermons, he and Frederick stressed that the millennial process, making the world better and better in preparation for Christ's return, was a step-by-step progression that had intensified some thirty years before with the rise of the Harmonist movement in Württemberg.[125] The Harmonists, they said, had cultivated Christian perfection at Harmony and New Harmony. Now it was time for the Sunwoman to move one last time to create the final stage of God's millennial plan, "the divine Economy." Their own perfection would be completed and Jesus Christ himself would come to dwell with them. As proof, the Harmonist prophet pointed to Revelation 21:3: "Behold, the tabernacle of God is with men, and he will dwell with them, and they shall be his people, and God himself shall be with them, and be their God." In an obscure analysis of this verse in his German Berlenburg Bible (*Berleburger*

Bibel), Rapp found the name for both this last millennial stage and his proposed new town. The Berlenburg commentary mentions "the correct Economy" ("*die recht Oekonomie*"). From this Rapp coined the phrase "the divine Economy" ("*die Gottliche Oekonomie*").[126] In his *Thoughts on the Destiny of Man,* he explained it as the culmination of the evolution of human nature in a divinely predestined system of spiritual, communal, and cosmic harmony.[127] The town where this perfect harmony would occur so Christ could appear would be named Economy (*Oekonomie*) and located twenty miles north of Pittsburgh on the Ohio River. By this move and this prophecy, Rapp hoped to resolve the challenges to his religious movement and its frontier community. He intended to solidify his patriarchal authority and ensure the prosperity of his Harmony Society. He would succeed in the latter goal but not the former.

In 1824, George Rapp entrusted Richard Flower with the awesome task of selling his whole town—the famous New Harmony on the Wabash with its nearly two hundred buildings and twenty thousand acres of land. The Harmonist leader had established a camaraderie with Morris Birkbeck and Richard's son George, the wealthy Englishmen who had co-founded Albion, Illinois, in 1817, across the Wabash in Edwards County. Birkbeck's earlier visit to New Harmony had helped convince him to locate his pioneering venture nearby. His *Notes on a Journey in America, from the Coast of Virginia to the Territory of Illinois,* which soon went through English, French, and German editions, included a favorable assessment of New Harmony that increased its international fame and served as an example to lure Englishmen to his Illinois settlement.[128] The German and English communities established a bond of mutual self-interest in a supply-and-demand arrangement that sustained what became known as the English Prairie of southern Illinois and, over the years, grossed $60,000 in sales for the Rappites.

Richard Flower advertised in newspapers of major American cities and as far distant as London, Paris, and Stuttgart. Then he journeyed all the way to New Lanark, Scotland, to meet a man wealthy enough and idealistic enough to consider such a deal. Flower already knew that Robert Owen, the owner and social reformer of this cotton mill town, admired the communal economic success of the Moravian, Shaker, and Harmonist settlements in America. That Owen also had read Morris Birkbeck's glowing account of New Harmony helped Flower convince him to cross the Atlantic Ocean and inspect this ready-made village for his projected model of a secular, socialistic New Moral World.[129]

While Flower searched for a buyer, the Harmonists gathered up their movable possessions. They reflected on their considerable economic, political, cultural, and spiritual achievements during their decade on the Wabash and began their departure. All of the nearly eight hundred would soon follow their sixty-six-year-old communal father, who left on the first boat. That very day, Lorenz Scheel wrote a prayer that can still be seen under the staircase of Community House No. 2: "On the twenty-fourth of May, 1824, we have departed. Lord, with Thy great help and goodness, in body and soul protect us." They fired the cannon, and the Harmonist prophet drifted off toward his divine Economy.

THE HARMONY SOCIETY AT ECONOMY, PENNSYLVANIA (1825–1905)

The Harmonist leader's move back to Pennsylvania did not hasten Christ's return or lessen tensions with his followers. Disenchanted members found it much easier to depart into the large German population of western Pennsylvania than into the wilds of the frontier. Certainly Father Rapp knew Jesus's caution that "of that day and hour knows no man, no, not the angels of heaven, but my Father only" (Matthew 24:36). Yet he let his acquaintance with the predictions of German clairvoyant Frederica Hauffe and his reading of millennial mystics overrule his biblical knowledge and

better judgment.[130] Making the mistake of many other would-be prophets, he went so far as to announce an exact date for the Savior's reappearance: September 15, 1829. The Swedish theologian Emanuel Swedenborg, whom Rapp read and admired, forecast that a new era was dawning and that a New Jerusalem would soon be a reality. Rapp knew that the German radical pietist Johann Heinrich Jung-Stilling had ventured into calculations of when these miraculous events would occur. So he was emboldened, believing himself entrusted with a formula involving his Harmony Society. As the Sunwoman in their American wilderness settlements, Rapp saw his Harmonists fulfilling Revelation 12:14: "And to the woman were given the two wings of a great eagle, that she might fly into the wilderness, into her place, where she is nourished for a time, and times, and half a time, from the face of the serpent." For Rapp it was all very logical. The largest contingent of Harmonists had arrived in America on September 15, 1804. Thus the scripture, he said, equated to the Harmonists' ten years at Harmony, ten at New Harmony, and the first five in their final town of Economy, north of Pittsburgh.[131]

The failure of Father Rapp's prediction left the determined Harmonist leader unshaken in his commitment to millennialism if not in the infallibility of his own prophetic powers. Yet this first failure was only one of several incidents that undermined Father Rapp's authority and further reduced his community. In a second lapse of judgment, he compromised his moral credibility by conducting experiments privately in his alchemy laboratory with a young and beautiful Harmonist, Hildegard Mutchler. He also exposed his mystical ineptitude by failing to produce the miraculous Philosopher's Stone to cure disease and turn base metal into gold. This third failing made him vulnerable to Bernhard Müller, a radical pietist who claimed to be Archduke Maximilian von Este, the illegitimate son of a German nobleman. Müller declared himself to be of the stem of Judah and root of David. As a self-proclaimed forerunner of Christ's return, if not the returning Savior himself, he was traveling under the assumed name Count de Leon, the Lion of Judah.

Providentially, in late September 1829, just after the failure of Father Rapp's prediction of Christ's return, he received a letter announcing the count's intention to come to America on a divine mission. Rapp, wanting to believe that Count de Leon was a possible fulfillment of his own prophecy, welcomed him to the community on October 18, 1831. Professing supernatural powers that Father Rapp obviously lacked, he divided the society and led the largest single departure of members in Harmonist history, called the Great Schism of 1832. In this schism, one-third left, 256 of the 771.[132] Conflicts over payment to these seceders brought Rapp to force another revision to the Articles of Agreement in 1836. He insisted upon deleting the guaranteed remunerations provided for in Article VI, which he had resented since 1808 when its inclusion had been mandated by the Pennsylvania legislature.[133]

One is left to wonder, however, whether the Harmonist leader ever realized the full impact of his Harmony Society on the communal tradition in America and beyond. The Great Schism itself scattered former Harmonists who followed new prophets and established new communities across the continent. Those who stayed with Count Leon set up the nearby New Philadelphia Society at Phillipsburg, now Monaca, Pennsylvania. By 1834, he had moved them to Louisiana, where some lived in the Grand Ecore and Germantown communities until 1871.[134] Other 1832 seceders believed enough in the supernatural powers of a Dr. Wilhelm Keil to build his communities at Bethel, Missouri, and Aurora, Oregon, which lasted into the 1880s.[135] From correspondence and direct interaction over the decades, George Rapp certainly realized how much influence his communal success must have had on the choice of both secular and religious movements to organize communally. The three principal socialist movements that established more

than sixty communal groups across the United States in the nineteenth century drew inspiration from the economic success of his Harmony Society—the Owenites of Robert Owen, Fourierists of Charles Fourier, and the Icarians of Etienne Cabet.[136] Father Rapp and other Harmonist leaders communicated and cooperated with nearly all of the major communal groups of their time, including the Shaker communities, the Zoarites of Ohio, and the Inspirationists of Iowa. The Harmony Society generously aided religious communitarians from the like-minded Hutterites of the Dakotas to celibate monastic Roman Catholics.[137] Since the millennial Rappites looked for the return of the Jews to Palestine as a sign of the end-times, in the 1870s and 1880s they sent significant sums of money to the Christian Zionist movement based in Württemberg. These funds assisted greatly in the founding of Zionist colonies with schools and hospitals in Haifa, Joppa, and Jerusalem.[138] Had the Harmonists survived long enough, they would have known that Jewish Zionists, some of whom may have been among those who cooperated with the German Christian Zionists, created the communal kibbutz movement that helped make Israel a Jewish nation.

Until the very day he died, on August 7, 1847, at age eighty-nine, the prophet George Rapp expected to complete his own millennial mission in the Holy Land. His final words were reported as "If I did not so fully believe that the Lord has designed me to place our society before his presence in the land of Canaan, I would consider this my last."[139] However, if Rapp's move from New Harmony did not fulfill his millennial promise, naming his third town Economy did act as a self-fulfilling prophecy by predicting the increasing economic prosperity of his Harmony Society. To outsiders who knew nothing of "the divine Economy," the town's name only implied the increasingly business-oriented direction of Rapp's peculiar movement. As head trustee, R. L. Baker would lead the Harmony Society to the pinnacle of its financial success. Father Rapp, having noticed the young Baker's precocious interest in economics as a schoolboy at New Harmony, chose him to apprentice with Frederick to learn "worldly wisdom" ("*Welt Weisheit*"). Baker became a trustee of the Harmony Society and was elected to direct its business affairs after Frederick died unexpectedly in 1834. Baker became president of the society and guided it from being a pioneer in American manufacturing to being a leader in American industry. The Harmony Society's investments in railroads, oil refineries, and its own oil pipeline helped bring the United States into the industrial age.[140]

Nevertheless, Economy's financial surge could not stop the decline in Harmony Society membership, made inevitable by celibacy, which caused it to be dissolved in 1905. In 1916, six acres containing Economy's principal buildings, gardens, and grounds became state property and are now known as Old Economy Vil-

lage, a National Historic Landmark—as are the historic sections of Harmony and New Harmony. Since the American Bridge Company had purchased 2,500 acres of Economy land for its steel plant in 1903, Economy was later renamed Ambridge. This company provided the steel for many of the most famous structures across America—California's San Francisco–Oakland Bay Bridge and New York's Verrazano-Narrows Bridge, Empire State Building, and Rockefeller Center.[141] It is altogether possible that the steel for the present bridge across the Wabash River at New Harmony was fabricated on land once part of Harmonist Economy. Curiously for a town founded by pacifists, one of major functions of this bridge, at the time the only span across the Wabash south of Vincennes, was to convey defense workers from southern Illinois to the LST plant in Evansville, Indiana during World War II. (See color plate, p. 82.)

THE OWENITES

OWENITE ORIGINS IN WALES, ENGLAND, AND SCOTLAND (1771–1824)

Robert Owen was already one of the most famous men in Britain when Richard Flower arrived at his cotton mill town trying to sell him New Harmony. It was the summer of 1824 in New Lanark, Scotland. Owen had risen from poverty to wealth to become a rare champion of the rights and well-being of the working classes at the beginning of the Industrial Revolution. He had already formulated his own theory of the New Moral World, a secular utopia of peace and plenty, truth and happiness.[1] He believed that the new social order could be realized by creating a superior character in each individual from birth and that the means were readily available to human hands. Loving care and a liberal education within the protective environment of socialistic communities of equality would lead inevitably to rational mental independence and universal human bliss. Once he learned of the financial success of George Rapp's Harmony Society and Ann Lee's Shakers, he became interested in creating a working model of the New Moral World in a communal setting.

Robert Owen's own character was molded as the sixth of seven children in a working-class family in Newtown, Wales. He was born on May 14, 1771, just five years before Britain's American colonies revolted against King George III in "the pursuit of happiness" which became the ultimate objective of Owen's own utopian crusade. Like most poor children caught in the early social distress of the Industrial Revolution, the young Owen faced but two options after his tenth birthday: he could work in a factory or seek an apprenticeship. At ten, he ended his formal education and moved to London, where his brother helped him become the apprentice of Mr. McGuffog, a prominent Scottish clothing fabric and dry goods merchant in Stamford, England. Owen's experiences in McGuffog's home and store gave direction to his thought and career. By his own testimony, he received kind treatment and averaged five hours a day reading books from his master's library.[2] In about 1787, just as machines and steam power were revolutionizing textile manufacturing, Owen left McGuffog's store with a thorough knowledge of textiles and their market potential.

He went off to seek his fortune in Manchester, the center of England's emerging textile industry. By his twentieth birthday, the young capitalist had parlayed borrowed money into a spinning machinery business and already managed the large Chorlton Twist Company. The very industrial system from which he would acquire his wealth was also creating the social degradation that

Robert Owen. Engraving of portrait by Matilda Heming, 1823.

Courtesy of the Robert Owen Museum, Newtown, Wales.

later touched his heart and fueled his social reform movement. In 1799, Owen made the decision that set the future course of his business and reform careers. With Manchester partners, he purchased the famous cotton-spinning mills of David Dale at New Lanark, Scotland, and assumed their management. Dale and Richard Arkwright, inventor of the water-frame spinning machine, had taken

advantage of the waterpower below the Falls of Clyde, about midway between Glasgow and Edinburgh, to complete the first massive stone mill in 1785, around which grew one of Britain's largest cotton-manufacturing villages. By adding row houses and schools, Dale attracted 1,500 workers to this remote factory town in the scenic but narrowly confining valley of the Clyde River.

In this isolated company town, Owen found a bride, an industrial fortune, and a ready-made laboratory for his social experiments. His hopes for both business profits and the eventual realization of the New Moral World rested on effective social control and character formation. The New Lanark labor community itself provided the prototype for the planned communities he announced in 1816 as a means for implementing his campaign on behalf of the poor and working classes. British Owenite historian John F. C. Harrison questions "whether Owen would have become a communitarian [at all] had he not been a cotton spinner." Harrison finds it clear that "the idea of the factory colony or community was closely associated with the early machine textile industry, which not only pioneered the technological changes of the first Industrial Revolution but also developed new forms of social organization." This supports his conclusion that "the model factory was the germ of Owen's communitarianism."[3]

In pursuit of the industrial fortune which had made him one of Britain's wealthiest entrepreneurs by the 1810s, Owen became captivated by the idea of a science of society. His interest was driven by a desire akin to that of other contemporary mill town owners, a good number of whom initiated projects for improvement among their own mill workers. Owen knew that factory production and village management depended on the health, well-being, and discipline of his poor villagers. In 1811, they numbered 2,206, of whom 1,360, mostly women and children, worked in the mills.[4] Thus, he was drawn to methods that promised social and behavioral control within the context of a community of workers about whose physi-

Robert Owen's New Lanark, Scotland, mill town with children lined up outside the Institute for the Formation of Character and workers dancing on the road. Sketch by John Winning, c. 1818.

Courtesy of the New Lanark Trust, New Lanark Mills, Scotland.

cal care and intellectual and cultural improvement he felt genuine concern. One of Owen's early innovations was a "silent monitor," a two-inch-long block of wood painted on four sides—black for "Excessive Naughtiness," blue for "A Neutral State of Morals," yellow for "Moderate Goodness," and white for "Super Excellence in Conduct." One block hung by each workstation in the mills for Owen and everyone else to see. The color on display indicated each employee's performance the previous day as rated by a foreman and recorded in a "book of character."[5]

Determined to maximize his control while ensuring a contented, efficient workforce, Owen came to view education as central to socialization. David Dale's schools were for children ages six to ten. Owen expanded this range downward to include infants and upward to provide lifelong learning for adults. After 1809, for a small fee, parents could place children as young as one year old in the new infant school. This not only freed mothers to work in the factory, like modern day-care centers, it also contributed to Owen's larger purpose of replacing negative family influence with a positive environment for instilling desired values and fashioning superior character. In effect, the infant school permitted the community to replace the family in matters of personal development and social control. The pioneering techniques Owen conceived for his infant and day schools soon aroused wide interest. Thousands of visitors from Europe and America inspected them. Nearly three decades before Friedrich Froebel began his *kindergarten* for German youngsters, Owen insisted that loving kindness with no contrived rewards or punishments permeate the New Lanark school system.

After 1813, Owen's new London partners, especially Quaker philanthropist William Allen and the well-known utilitarian philosopher Jeremy Bentham, insisted upon introducing the popular method of Englishman Joseph Lancaster that held the promise of literacy and knowledge for all. As used in New Lanark and as far away as the Shaker and Harmonist communities in America, Lancaster's system designated students as monitors to teach other students what they themselves had learned by rote. However, Owen wanted textbooks used sparingly. Students learned mostly by doing, in a style used in the school of Johann Heinrich Pestalozzi, a progressive educator in Switzerland. Owen sent all four of his sons to the Pestalozzian-style school of Philip Emanuel von Fellenberg in Hofwyl, Switzerland. Children in New Lanark learned through play, conversation, singing, dancing, and military-style marching. The playground was as important as the classroom. Huge maps and giant pictures of animals graced the walls of one room in the New Lanark school, where geography was taught by a game. Owen required teachers to consider the needs and maturation levels of their charges and to tailor their methods accordingly, always starting with the familiar and progressing to the unfamiliar and the abstract.[6]

The New Lanark educational system was complete when Owen opened his Institution for the Formation of Character in 1816. The name itself proclaimed the comprehensive purpose of his entire program of education. This single institution combined under one roof his infant and day schools and introduced educational, social, and cultural activities for adults. Lectures, discussions, and debates addressed subjects from natural science to ancient history. The older residents became part of the captive audience in Owen's company town. Every event designed for them lent itself to adult education, recreation, or indoctrination in Owen's emerging utopian theories.

When the effectiveness of these methods became apparent, Robert Owen gained a reputation for efficient, benevolent factory management. He soon distinguished himself beyond his fellow industrialists, even the socially conscious ones such as David Dale who tried similar progressive policies regarding wages, working hours, and education. Owen's keen sensitivity to the plight of poor workers injected a moral dimension into his thinking about poverty and riches existing side by side in the industrial age. He recognized and freely admitted that society's increase in wealth during the Napoleonic era, as well as his own, was not created by his or others' advanced managerial skills but rather by the productivity of new machinery. He argued that if human beings were organized and serviced as carefully as the machines they operated all employers would profit. But regardless of their profit or loss, Owen accepted the social responsibility of owners and managers to the working classes, a view that placed him outside the circle of other cotton spinners and beyond the capitalistic ideas of classical economists such as Adam Smith. Owen's ideas were closer to the socialist economic theories of David Ricardo. As early as 1812, Owen the industrialist became a public propagandist for his radical ideas.[7]

The cotton spinner of New Lanark summarized his advanced economic views in a *Report to the County of Lanark* in 1820. He argued that since manual labor is the source of all wealth, laborers

Classroom of Robert Owen's school at New Lanark, Scotland. Watercolor by G. Hunt, 1820s.

Courtesy of the New Lanark Trust, New Lanark Mills, Scotland.

can properly claim their fair share. In planned agricultural and manufacturing villages of cooperation, Owen saw the potential for production that so far exceeded consumption that "each may be freely permitted to receive from the general store of the community whatever they may require."[8] He always held that both communal property and social equality were contingent upon unlimited production. In reality, as long as the Old Immoral World of superstition, prejudice, and greed endured in the general society, Owen's words in support of social and economic equality went far beyond his will or ability to implement them, even in a "community of equality" of his own making.

At first, his speeches and writings were aimed at finding like-minded New Lanark partners and securing national labor legislation. Then he looked for philanthropic industrialists to erect model industrial villages for both social improvement and personal profit.[9] These self-sufficient communities of 500 to 1,500 residents would benefit paupers and the greatly expanding ranks of the unemployed by providing jobs and housing at the close of the Napoleonic Wars. During the Great Depression of the 1930s, the New Deal Community Program of the United States government set up somewhat similar voluntary settlements for the unemployed in thirty-two states.[10]

By 1817, Owen had published ideas that committed his movement to a well-defined communitarian program for the much broader, utopian purpose of reorganizing the entire society for the emancipation of mankind. He made serious efforts to bring his plan to the attention of the most powerful people in high places, including heads of state, in Britain and beyond. Later, he ambitiously claimed that these writings were "intended to effect an entire revolution in the spirit, mind, manners, habits, and conduct of the human race;—a rational, practical revolution, to be introduced gradually, in peace, with wise foresight, and to be highly beneficial for all."[11] He personally handed all the reigning sovereigns at the 1818 Congress of Aix-la-Chapelle copies of his scheme in three languages. Czar Alexander I of Russia, whose clothing fit so tightly he had no pockets, refused a copy saying, "I cannot receive it—I have no place to put it in."[12] Thus, the utopian from New Lanark missed whatever chance he had to gain support from the czar for his New Moral World—the same ruler who would provide land for Württemberg millennialists in the Caucasus.[13] In 1822 and 1823, Owen made speaking tours to Ireland. He persisted in laying his village plan before committees of Parliament until, in May 1824, his best friend in the legislature, Sir William de Crespigny, respectfully requested that he not bring up the matter again. No government, philanthropist, or industrialist stepped forward with any funding to test his communal plan.

Equal to Owen's utopian benevolence ranked his aggressive paternalism. At New Lanark, he instituted curfews, random body searches to prevent theft, and fines for drunkenness or for having children out of wedlock. He established committees for house inspections—somewhat as Henry Ford did much later in Detroit. These strategies aroused conflict. Enraged ladies in New Lanark called inspectors the "Bug Hunters" and "military police" and often refused to open their doors. Although Owen cast himself in the role of chief advocate for the interests of the masses, he never considered them his equals. He spoke with condescending certainty about the brutal ignorance and stupidity of the common people and equated making them happy with making them docile.[14] In 1816, he firmly asserted that he did not wish "to have the opinions of the ill-trained and uninformed on any of the measures intended for their relief and amelioration. No! On such subjects, until they shall be instructed in better habits, and made rationally intelligent, their advice can be of no value."[15]

The beginnings of Owenism as a distinct, nonsectarian movement had become evident as early as 1812. In that year Owen's original partners, tired of the distractions and expense of his social reform efforts, had fired him from his managerial position in the New Lanark mills. If this had not occurred, he might never have started writing the calls for reform that came to define his movement. Character formation was its fundamental principle and improvement of conditions for the unemployed and working poor its practical goal.[16] He was forced to seek out genuine reform advocates, including Jeremy Bentham, with whom he repurchased the mills and regained his managerial position in 1813. During his months scouting for partners in London, Owen used his first anonymous pamphlet, *Statement Regarding the New Lanark Establishment* (1812), to begin defining his theories, achievements, and plans. From that time forward, with the encouragement of his new business associates, he looked increasingly outward from his New Lanark base to achieve reforms of national and, eventually, international scope. He proclaimed that the solutions already found in his own small, self-contained mill community were capable of solving the universal problems of poverty, unemployment, and ignorance in industrial society.

In 1799, when Robert Owen purchased David Dale's spinning mills, he also married Dale's daughter, Ann Caroline. Contrary to his own growing animosity to established religion, which he equated with oppressive superstition, his wife was steeped in her father's Protestant fundamentalism and millennialism. Owen disdained the belief in the second coming of Christ to effect a better world that so possessed his wife and much of the churchgoing public in Britain. Yet, after 1817, he incorporated a secular form of millennialism into his own reform propaganda, and often quoted biblical passages to reinforce his arguments.[17] During his apprenticeship with McGuffog, he had gradually relinquished the Christian faith he had learned at home. In its place came a rational and eclectic approach to ethics and morality with an abiding skepticism of the motives and doctrines of organized religion. Perhaps inevitably, Ann and Robert grew apart over religious and other matters. Their

separation became complete when he sailed to America in 1824, and he did not attend her funeral in 1831, even though he was in England when she died.

After 1817, when Owen began expressing these unorthodox views in public attacks on the abuses of the clergy and the injustices of marriage as tied to religion, he discovered that this drew far more criticism and did more damage to his appeal than all his radical economic theories and community-building schemes. Yet he could not contain his unorthodoxy. In America, he was widely castigated after using his speech in New Harmony on July 4, 1826, the fiftieth anniversary of the Declaration of Independence, to make his own "Declaration of Mental Independence." He praised the American Revolution as the first opportunity to use political power to attack the "Trinity" of evils: "PRIVATE, OR INDIVIDUAL PROPERTY—ABSURD AND IRRATIONAL SYSTEMS OF RELIGION—AND MARRIAGE, FOUNDED ON INDIVIDUAL PROPERTY COMBINED WITH SOME ONE OF THESE IRRATIONAL SYSTEMS OF RELIGION."[18] Many in America unfairly branded him and his movement as atheistic. Yet Owen, like other rationalistic deists of his time, such as Benjamin Franklin and Thomas Jefferson, reasoned "that there is an external or an internal cause of all existences, by the fact of their existence; [and] that this all-pervading cause of motion and change in the universe, is that Incomprehensible Power, which the nations of the world have called God."[19] Eventually, Owen proposed a universal "Rational Religion" within a "Rational System of Society" based on the idea that "truth is nature, and nature God; that God is truth, and truth is God."[20]

Although Robert Owen always asserted that his lofty ideas were original, born of his own experience and intuition, his approach to the social problems of the industrial age did not originate in an intellectual vacuum. During his entire career, he rarely missed an opportunity to turn an idea that caught the popular imagination into a reason to believe in the truth of his own crusade, from socialism and communalism to millennialism, spiritualism, and phrenology. His thoughts and actions clearly identify him with the Enlightenment rationalism of the late eighteenth and early nineteenth centuries, which expressed concern over the social effects of industrialization and called for social planning to improve living conditions and even to perfect human character. Owen's voracious reading at McGuffog's, his association in the 1790s with the Literary and Philosophical Society in Manchester, and his membership in the Glasgow Literary and Commercial Society after 1800 gave him opportunity to begin absorbing these modern concepts. During his quarter century at New Lanark, he became acquainted with noted social theorists William Godwin, Jeremy Bentham, and James Mill. Owen's private conversations with them and his familiarity with their published works affected his own thinking, as did the writings of Jean-Jacques Rousseau and other Enlightenment figures. He borrowed directly from some of them. Perhaps the most obvious influence is Godwin's *An Enquiry concerning Political Justice* (1793), which is reflected in Owen's 1813 *A New View of Society,* the first printed summary of his ideas. However, where Godwin's new social order called for justice, equality, and freedom for the individual, Owen stressed the achievement of human happiness with fulfillment in body, mind, and spirit but under managed conditions.[21] One London critic, William Hazlitt, took offense at Owen's calling his view of society "new." He insisted that "it is as old as the *Political Justice* of Mr. Godwin, as the Oceana of [James] Harrington, as the *Utopia* of Sir Thomas More, as the *Republic* of Plato."[22]

Owen and his movement also were closely associated with the earliest attempts to place the understanding and control of the individual and society on a scientific footing. He became friends with several Scottish moral philosophers and political economists at the University of Glasgow and University of Edinburgh who were seeking bases for what eventually emerged as the behavioral sciences. Many Owenite converts who thought deeply about solutions for the problems of industrial society first became interested in behavioral science as a result of Owen's impassioned call for a science of society.[23] Behaviorism was the core of the "Great Truth" of the ages which Owen naively claimed as his own personal revelation. He referred to this truth as the messiah that had come to mankind through him: "It is of all truths the most important, that the character of man is formed FOR—not BY himself."[24] Therefore, Owen claimed, "Any general character, from the best to the worst, from the most ignorant to the most enlightened, may be given to any community, even to the world at large, by the application of proper means; which means are to a great extent at the command and under the control of those who have influence in the affairs of men."[25]

This theme dominated Owen's thought and plans from 1813 onward. It became evident when he chose "Essays on the Principle of the Formation of Human Character" as a subtitle for his *A New View of Society,* which he published that year. And it continued through his last summary of his theories, a collection of essays he wrote between 1836 and 1844 and published as *The Book of the New Moral World.* This assumption that individuals, communities, and the world could be improved by the intentional formation of character underlay all of Owen's efforts. Everything else he tried—in education, legislation, secular millennialism, philanthropy, and building whole villages of unity and mutual cooperation—was a means to this end.

Before he adopted the laborious and expensive method of creating whole communities, Owen tried gradual reform. He opted first for the legislative route. He directed his energies toward convincing Parliament to enact nationally some features of his own enlightened factory management. These included forbidding child labor under age ten, requiring four years of schooling before a child could be employed, and restricting work to ten and a half hours per day for children under eighteen. However, Owen soon grew frustrated with the slow pace of legislative reform. Not until 1819 did he see any legislation result from his efforts, and then it came with dishearteningly reduced provisions. Only the Factory Act of 1833, passed long after he had given up lobbying Parliament, came close to his recommendations. Owen finally turned to the community-building alternative. He felt this promised more immediate and complete results than either gradual reform or providing assistance to individuals.[26] Also, he thought, it would preclude the kind of violent revolution that had shaken France. On New Year's Day 1816, the master of New Lanark dramatically announced this new direction for the next phase of Owenism at the opening of his Institution for the Formation of Character.

If the British factory town provided the prototype for Owen's idea of building entire new communities to redeem the working classes and shape human character, the communally organized settlements of the Shakers of Mother Ann Lee and Harmonists of Father George Rapp supplied the proof that such communities could be practical and economically successful. In the 1810s and early 1820s, Owen's growing familiarity with their settlements in America convinced him to pursue the complicated communal method of social reform. In 1774, a decade before Owen's arrival in Manchester, Ann Lee, who claimed to be a millennial female Christ, escaped that city's dehumanizing factories and religious constraints by emigrating to America with her small band of Shakers. Owen monitored their communal progress, and by 1815 he also knew of George Rapp's millennial German communities at Harmony and New Harmony. His Edinburgh friend George Courtauld kept him abreast of both Harmonist progress and the rapid western expansion of the Shaker communities. In 1816, the Philadelphia Quaker W. S. Warder passed direct information about the Shakers to Owen that he printed in 1817 as *A Brief Sketch of the*

Religious Society of People Called Shakers.[27] By this time, he was convinced that the Shakers were achieving goals he had set for his own New Lanark: social discipline, breaking down family ties to serve the common good, and becoming self-sufficient through agriculture, high-quality handicrafts, and fair dealing. So he gladly began to point to Shaker villages as proof that communal organization could mold character and solve basic economic and social problems. By 1820, he wrote to the Harmony Society to learn their methods of successfully operating New Harmony; he sent them his publications and requested theirs.[28]

Consequently, when Richard Flower arrived in 1824 offering Owen an opportunity to buy New Harmony, circumstances had already conspired to favor the sale. Owen found that personal, business, and managerial problems in New Lanark made it remarkably easy for him to set aside those responsibilities in order to devote all his time to his new social reform career. His marriage was contentious. His pious business partners were so upset with his public stand against established religion and a report that he had banned the Bible from New Lanark that they forced him to revise his prized school program and threatened to relieve him of his directorship of the mills. Even his normally congenial relations with his own employees were in disarray. He had impounded the assets of their benefit fund and frequently absented himself from his mill town as a general wage controversy swept the Scottish cotton industry. An outbreak of typhoid fever suggested that Owen had exaggerated his claims for hygiene and housing in the village. Two books appeared claiming that social conditions in some other mill towns at least equaled those instituted by Owen in New Lanark.[29]

OWENITE NEW HARMONY (1825–1827)

When Owen, at age fifty-three, sailed from Liverpool for America in October 1824, he tried to leave his New Lanark problems completely behind. He did not return until 1827, and by 1829 he had sold all his interests there; for the rest of his long life, he lived on a modest annuity. On the Indiana frontier, he imagined, he could begin a new community process that would achieve for the entire human race the happiness that he could not find even for himself in New Lanark. Mercifully perhaps, his utopian vision blinded him to how inadequately his New Lanark experiences had prepared him for administering the first model community for his, or any, secular social movement. When he reached New Harmony on December 17, 1824, he virtually had made up his mind to purchase the town. He had paused twice during his whirlwind tour of the East to make his first visits to functioning utopian villages. He spent several hours with the Shakers at Niskayuna (Watervliet) near Albany, New York, on November 11 and stayed overnight with the Harmonists at their partially built third town of Economy, north of Pittsburgh on the Ohio River, on December 4 and 5.[30] According to the accounts of Owen's traveling partners, his youngest son, William, and his Scottish friend Donald Macdonald, he and George Rapp had a meeting of minds, or as near to that as could be expected from widely differing charismatic leaders. William noted in his diary:

> Mr. Owen conversed a long time with Mr. Rapp. He explained the formation of character and many of the results deduced from it. Mr. Rapp appeared to agree to all of it. Indeed, he said he had long thought so too. He seemed much pleased to find an individual with whom he had so many ideas in common. He said he had often exclaimed to himself "My God! is there no man on God's earth who has the same opinions as myself and can help me in my plans? I am now lucky to have come in contact with such an one."[31]

Much of this commodious goodwill might be attributed to the lateness of the hour, the good wine, and the pending sale. Once in New Harmony, it took Owen only a scant eighteen days to inspect the town and visit the nearby English settlement of Morris Birkbeck and George Flower in Albion, Illinois, across the Wabash. By January 3, 1825, he and Frederick Rapp, George's adopted son, concluded the $135,000 deal. In total, Owen would expend $200,000 of his $250,000 fortune on his New Harmony project many times this amount in today's dollars.[32] Even this was a bargain compared to the seven-hundred-acre communal village he had earlier contemplated for Motherwell, near Glasgow, which would have taken double Owen's resources.[33]

Robert Owen's four sons and one daughter who followed him to America actively embraced their father's visionary humanitarianism. As well-educated individuals, they played vital roles as loyal practitioners and articulate exponents of his utopian ideals. William accompanied his father to New Harmony in 1824. Although only twenty-two years old, he and Owen's faithful Scottish friend Donald Macdonald became the initial managers of New Harmony while the elder Owen took a public relations tour all the way back to England. Eldest son Robert Dale arrived in New Harmony in January 1826 with Philadelphia scientists and educators aboard the keelboat his father dubbed the Boatload of Knowledge. David Dale and Richard arrived in January 1828. Daughter Jane Dale came in 1833 after the deaths of her mother and two sisters. This involvement of Owen's children is of special importance. After the first wave of Owenite community building abated in 1829, Owen's children extended the effective life of Owenism in America by translating their father's utopian dreams into the crusades for women's rights, birth control, tax-supported public schools, and freedom for the slaves.

On April 27, 1825, the utopian from New Lanark officially opened New Harmony for community life to all who would accept his generous, if nebulous, offer to make it their home under an economic arrangement yet to be determined. This turned out to be an unsatisfactory use of leases—from which some later suspected that Owen might profit—rather than individual deeds to New

William Owen.
Attributed to David
Dale Owen.

*From the Collection
of the Indiana
State Museum and
Historic Sites.*

to the individual selfish system and all seem prepared . . . to give up the latter and adopt the former. In fact the whole of this country is ready to commence a new empire upon the principle of public property and to discard private property."[35] But he bluntly announced to those gathered in the former Harmonist brick church that "as no other individual has had the same experience as myself in the practice of the system about to be introduced, I must for some time, partially take the lead in its direction."[36] He unwittingly helped sink his flagship project of communitarian socialism by thinking of the majority of its American farmer and mechanic volunteers as he had the poor, submissive residents of his Scottish mill town. Reflecting upon the grave difficulties a manager turned philanthropist confronted in administering a community filled with eight or nine hundred freedom-loving, backwoods Americans, his wealthy Scottish colleague William Maclure later observed that Owen had failed to recognize "the materials in this country are not the same as the cotton spinners at New Lanark, nor does the advice of a patron go so far."[37]

In America, Owen stood at center stage with a unique opportunity to communicate and demonstrate a plan to transform the human character and condition. The extent to which the "social father" met this challenge defines the degree to which Owenite communitarian socialism affected the direction of American social history. Unfortunately, in at least three respects, he carried his least productive approaches to reform in Scotland into the quite different American arena, where they became injurious to his movement and to the first important nonsectarian community scheme in the country. Unnecessary criticism, wasted time, and communal dysfunction resulted.

First, Owen continued to attack established religion, an indulgence that had driven away even his reform-minded business partners. Seemingly oblivious to America's constitutional guarantees of religious freedom and separation of church and state, he

Harmony property.[34] Nevertheless, since it was already famous as a Harmony Society communal village, New Harmony rapidly overflowed with new residents attracted by Owen's open invitation. Its 180 buildings included dwellings and community houses for eight hundred people, two churches, four mills, numerous shops, a textile factory, tan yard, distillery, and brewery. These plus vineyards, orchards, and two thousand acres under cultivation seemed ideally suited for the beginning of his utopian dream. He optimistically declared that "the United States but particularly the States west of the Allegheny Mountains have been prepared in the most remarkable manner for the New System. The principle of union and cooperation . . . is now universally admitted to be far superior chose to attack the faith of others rather than to assert his own right to gain a legitimate following for his own unorthodox deistic Rational Religion. In 1828, a year after New Harmony ceased to be an Owenite community, its apostle of rationalism was still baiting the Christian clergy. From New Orleans, he issued a general challenge for a clergyman to defend the merits of religion in an open debate. The sharp-witted Alexander Campbell, later a co-founder of the Disciples of Christ Church, accepted the challenge. Capacity crowds of twelve hundred attended fifteen public sessions in Cincinnati in April 1829. Owen courteously presented his Twelve Laws to disprove Christianity and tried "to Prove That the Principles of All Religions Are Erroneous, and That Their Practice Is Injurious to the Human Race."[38] By Campbell's count, at the conclusion only three people stood to indicate they found Owen's arguments convincing.[39] Christians interpreted this as an encouraging sign from a region of the country not particularly known for its piety. Owen, knowing by then that New Harmony and fourteen of the fifteen other Owenite-type communities begun by others in the United States and Britain had passed out of existence, took the result of the debate as a cue to return to England.[40] There, from 1829 to 1834, according to the British Owen scholar John Harrison, he and his readily adaptable reform movement sought "a fresh approach, using new institutions and agencies."[41] Owen did not return to the United States until 1844. By that time a new generation of reformers had sparked a revival of interest in his communitarian socialism but not in his religious radicalism.[42]

A second and unsuspected liability for Owen was his stubborn attachment to rationalist Enlightenment concepts. This both gained and lost his movement devotees in the United States. His appeal to familiar Enlightenment themes placed him in the American tradition of Benjamin Franklin, John Adams, Thomas Jefferson, and Thomas Paine. This attracted a few liberal-leaning

persons to backwoods Indiana to help Owen begin his new "Social System." These included the social reformer William Maclure, the feminist Frances Wright, and the radical egalitarian Paul Brown. Such individuals already supported natural rights, environmental determinism, women's rights, and deism. However, Owen's appeal to Enlightenment thought proved to be a liability in attempting to attract independent Jeffersonian farmers. They had shelved deism and adopted the revivalism and evangelicalism that flowed from the camp meetings of the Second Great Awakening, which had been held on the frontier since the turn of the century. This same revival of religion brought the Shakers to Kentucky, Ohio, and Indiana. Thus, as Harrison concludes, "When contemporaries charged Owenites with infidelity the condemnation implied that they were not only godless but also out of date."[43]

Owen's third difficulty in America related to the second. Whenever he had to choose whether to direct his message to the upper or lower classes, he chose the upper, as he always had in Europe. He continued to believe, although all his European experience indicated to the contrary, that the wealthy and politically powerful would bless his designs with their philanthropy and legislation. Although between 1824 and 1829, he laid his plans before many individual congressmen and twice in speeches in the Hall of Representatives at the Capitol in Washington, he neither requested nor received any specific legislation or funding. If William Maclure, a Scottish merchant who made his fortune in international trade and sought social reform through progressive education, had not reluctantly become his investment partner in New Harmony, Owen's attention to potential philanthropists would have paid no dividends either.

Yet Owen's first three and a half weeks in America before he headed west on November 28 can only be described as a triumphal entry. Few other visitors to the United States had experienced such a grand reception. In New York, Philadelphia, and Washington, his reputation as one of Britain's wealthiest industrialists and the benevolent manager of the New Lanark mills won him invitations from not only President James Monroe, Secretary of State John Adams, John C. Calhoun, and other congressmen but also from notable industrialists, aristocrats, and state officials who welcomed him at their dinners and sometimes applauded his message. Jeremiah Thompson, who started the first line of transatlantic packet ships, held a dinner in Owen's honor that was attended by mercantile and shipping magnates. Dinner invitations came from the New York governor, Joseph Yates, and the governor-elect, DeWitt Clinton.[44]

Upper-class reformers and intellectuals in New York and Philadelphia, part of a small but growing band of Owen enthusiasts, received him as the practical guide to a new moral age. The New York Society for Promoting Communities welcomed him the day he arrived in America. This organization, founded in 1820, had printed parts of his *A New View of Society* in 1822 along with John Melish's account of the Harmony Society. Such groups already concerned about social justice and anxious to imitate Harmonist and Shaker success in nonsectarian forms found in Owen's systematic theory and charismatic leadership the final ingredients to inspire communal experimentation. In the next three decades, they would try his formula as well as those of French communitarian socialists Charles Fourier and Etienne Cabet.[45] Owen's ideas had filtered through since 1817 in comments upon his writings by major British reviews. An Owenite society soon formed in Philadelphia after excerpts from *A New View of Society* made their American debut that same year in the town's Jeffersonian newspaper, *Aurora*. Members of this society, such as Dutch scientist Gerard Troost, also belonged to the Academy of Natural Sciences of Philadelphia. Its president was William Maclure, whose mercantile fortune financed a second

William Maclure.

Courtesy of the New Harmony Working Men's Institute.

career that made him the "Father of American Geology." Scientists and educators from these two organizations and from Maclure's Pestalozzian school in Philadelphia became Owen's most devoted supporters from the educated class in America.

Madame Marie Duclos Fretageot, assistant in Maclure's school in Paris, brought an account of Owen's educational ideas with her when she came to direct Maclure's Philadelphia school in 1821. She apparently also introduced academy scientists to the educational and communitarian sides of Owenism. Troost and other academy members projected a community of their own by the fall of 1823 but, after meeting the magnetic Mr. Owen, decided to join his grander effort in New Harmony. Maclure showed some interest in the educational implications of a Philadelphia community project and had been favorably impressed by his visit with Owen in New Lanark in the summer of 1824. Nevertheless, it took the optimistic urging of Fretageot and a personal visit from Owen in Philadelphia in November 1825 to convince the wealthy former merchant that the New Harmony venture held enough promise to warrant the commitment of his considerable financial, educational, and scientific resources.[46]

Not until 1825, when he needed recruits from the ranks of the working classes to populate his experimental community in the backwoods, did Robert Owen, this cultivator of America's most influential leaders, find himself compelled to turn his attention toward its common people. Only then did he start to appreciate the power beginning to accumulate in their hands. He had never seemed to have pondered why, after freeing themselves from British royalty, the Americans had rejected both nobility and aristocratic privilege by denying all use of hereditary titles. And he never came to grips with the fact that Jeffersonian and Jacksonian democracy were bestowing voting, office-holding, and economic rights upon adult, white, property-less males. He also seems never to have perceived the depths of the leveling process in religion, sparked after 1795 by the Second Great Awakening, which lingered in the attitude and behavior of the upland southerners and backwoodsmen who joined New Harmony and helped to bring it down.

In the fiery emotion of the frontier camp meetings, the elitist Calvinistic doctrine that only a small number of "the elect" would be saved was transmuted into the more egalitarian concept of "whosoever will may be saved." Owen, his communitarian plan, and his animosity toward religion were ambushed in the backcountry by this rising importance of the common people in America.

In New Harmony, Owen discovered he could not create a "community of equality" that implied imposing the cultural and living standards of eastern seaboard reformers, educators, and scientists of "the better sort" upon the western farmers, mechanics, laborers, and artisans of "the common sort."[47] The separation and sometimes animosity between the classes gave the community an impersonal character. Paul Brown, the egalitarian purist, who registered this and many other complaints in his later *Twelve Months in New Harmony*, observed that the community was "void of all intimacy regarding each other's feelings, views and situation, including often their names."[48] Disdain for others grew at both ends of New Harmony's social ladder. Mrs. Sarah Pears, among those who migrated from Philadelphia, exclaimed, "Oh, if you could see some of the rough uncouth creatures here, I think you would find it hard to look on them in the light of brothers and sisters. . . . I am sure I cannot in sincerity look upon these as equals."[49] Karl Bernhard, the visiting duke of Saxe-Weimar-Eisenach, noticed the class division and wrote, "We collected together in the house No. 2 . . . where all the young ladies and gentlemen of *quality* assembled. In spite of the equality so much recommended, this class of persons will not mix with the common sort, and I believe that all the well brought up members are disgusted, and will soon abandon the society. We amused ourselves exceedingly during the whole remainder of the evening dancing cotillions, reels, and waltzes."[50]

Yet the working people in New Harmony refused to assume a position of deference, insignificance, or inferiority, unlike those

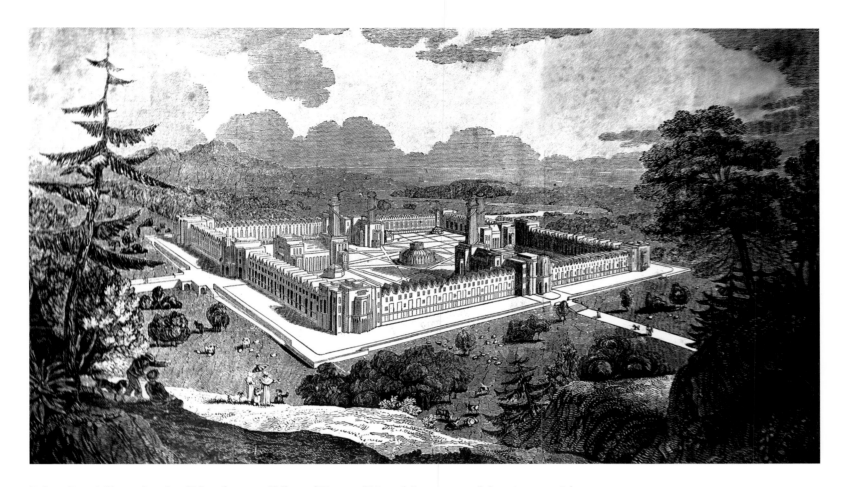

Robert Owen's "Agricultural and Manufacturing Village of Unity and Mutual Co-operation," the primary social unit for his utopian New Moral World. Design by English architect Stedman Whitwell, 1825.

in New Lanark, and therefore held the key to the very survival of Owen's experiment. They harbored a resentment that must be calculated into the division and collapse of the Owenite community.[51] The farmers and mechanics objected that their labors received a lower exchange value in "labor notes" at the communal store than that of the educators and scientists. They preferred their own music, dances, foods, drink, table manners, courting rituals, and speech to the sophisticated standards, including an official dress for men and women, set for them by Owen, Maclure, and their eastern recruits.[52] Holiday celebrations seem to have been the rare occasions when the classes laid aside their differences and found a degree of harmony. To the usual seasonal observances, including a Fourth of July tradition that continues to the present (see color plates, pp. 148–49), they added two of their own: Thomas Paine's birthday and the anniversary of the Battle of New Orleans. The latter became a joyous occasion for a splendid ball, military music, ringing bells, firing the cannon, and drinking intoxicated toasts like "May the light of Truth continue to emanate, and at length shine out so refulgent, that Error shall fly trembling before it."[53]

As discontent grew among both classes, Robert Owen continued to hold out the promise that New Harmony represented merely a temporary springboard to the ideal quadrangular towns he envisioned being built all over the world. In his mind, the economic, social, and cultural benefits of the New Moral World could only be fully realized in the idyllic environment of these "Agricultural and Manufacturing Villages of Unity and Mutual Cooperation." He used the promise that the first of these would soon be under construction three miles south of New Harmony much as Father Rapp had used the nearness of Christ's second coming to motivate his weary and restless Harmonists. The towns of the New Moral World were to be built on a grand scale according to designs Owen had had engraved and printed as early as 1817.[54] During his brief return to England in 1825, he optimistically hired architect Stedman Whitwell to build a detailed six-foot-square model of his ideal village. Returning to New York in November, the innovative reformer proudly displayed this representation of his intended communal masterpiece in public meetings there. After holding repeated showings in Philadelphia, including one at Charles Willson Peale's famous museum, he had Whitwell and Donald Macdonald take the model to the White House, where they explained its utopian purpose to President John Quincy Adams.[55] On December 6, 1825, the Washington *National Intelligencer* gave it very favorable

notice.[56] Although this model embodied the dream of the waiting residents, no record exists that Whitwell and Macdonald brought this hard-to-transport item to New Harmony. In fact, this object, one of the grand artifacts in all utopian history, somehow disappeared, just as surely as the hope of seeing the model rise in reality south of town.

In Owen's mind, each of his ideal communities was to feature a gigantic structure built in the form of a quadrangle, a parallelogram one thousand feet on a side and set on a plot of about thirty-three acres with outlying mills, factories, and farmlands. Dwellings resembling the row houses of New Lanark formed the walls enclosing the quadrangle, offering housing with gas lighting and hot and cold running water for two thousand residents. Everything imaginable was to be included for their comfort and enlightenment—from kitchens, dining halls, baths, laundries, and stores to schools, a library, museum, botanic gardens, gymnasiums, music rooms, and dance and lecture halls. When the noted German-American writer Charles Sealsfield discovered Owen's design during his visit to Indiana, he reported that "a plan was shown and sold to us, according to which a new building of colossal dimensions is projected; and if Mr. Owen's means should not fall short of his good will, this edifice would certainly exhibit the most magnificent piece of architecture in the Union, [only] the Capitol at Washington excepted. This palace, when finished, is to receive his community [from New Harmony]."[57] Owen promised the citizens of New Harmony that the first utopian town-in-a-garden would soon be theirs to enjoy "on the high lands of Harmony from 2 to 4 miles from the [Wabash] river and its island of which the occupants will have a beautiful and interesting view."[58] In fact, 240,000 bricks were fired at the proposed site, near present-day Springfield, where a few broken ones can still be found. In August 1825, William Pelham, editor of the *New-Harmony Gazette,* wrote optimistically to his son that "in 2 *years*, the contemplated new village will be ready for the reception of members."[59]

This Village of Unity and Mutual Cooperation was to be where the followers of Owen's vision would fully reap its amazing benefits, rather than in Harmonist-built New Harmony. This was intended as the first realization of an operating socialistic community to be replicated everywhere around the globe. It was similar to, but not to be mistaken for, the joint-stock communities proposed by Owen's contemporary, the French communalist Charles Fourier. Owen knew Fourier proposed settlements he called "phalanxes," each with a huge communal building known as a "phalanstery." Fourier predicted that exactly 2,985,984 phalanxes would one day thrive worldwide, and more than thirty, including Brook Farm, were attempted in the United States.[60] Owen never projected a total number of his quadrangular parallelograms, but he did envision them dotting every countryside, their fields, factories, and mills providing their citizens with all the necessities of life. Acting in perfect concert for their mutual prosperity, sharing their superior products on the basis of need rather than profit, these sharing and caring communities were to achieve abundance for all and thus the disappearance of private property and social inequality. As the "Great Truth" of character formation ultimately triumphed along with these communitarian developments, all humanity would attain Owen's ultimate utopian objective of happiness.

As Owen imagined:

> In these happy villages of unity, when disease or death assail their victim, every aid is near; all the assistance that skill, kindness, and sincere affection can invent, aided by every convenience and comfort, are at hand. . . . [They] have consolation in the certain knowledge that within their own immediate circle they have many, many others remaining; and around them on all sides, as far as the eye can reach, or imagination extend, thousands on thousands, in strict, intimate, and close union, are ready and willing to offer them aid and consolation.

> . . . Here may it be truly said, "O death, where is thy sting? O grave, where is thy victory?"[61]

Even the experience of terminal illness and death would lose the terror and grief they held during the individual isolation of the Old Immoral World. Owen had come to believe that in the New Moral World the average life span would be extended to as many as 140 years.[62] Everyone would enjoy not only a longer life but also a regenerated spirit. In Owen's words:

> This second creation or regeneration of man will bring forth in him new combinations of his natural faculties, qualities, and powers which will imbue him with a new spirit, and create in him new feelings, thoughts, and conduct, the reverse of those which have been hitherto produced. . . . This re-created or new-formed man will be enabled easily to subdue the earth, and make it an ever-varying paradise, the fit abode of highly intellectual moral beings, each of whom, for all practical purposes, will be the free possessor and delighted enjoyer of its whole extent; and that joy will be increased a thousand-fold, because all his fellow-beings will equally enjoy it with him.[63]

How remarkable that Owen's conception of a secularly produced "re-created or new-formed man" should provide one of the most intriguing connections between New Harmony "then and now." Paul Tillich, the noted twentieth-century German-American theologian and advocate of Christian socialism, became fascinated by Owen's ideas and the Harmonist and Owenite communal experiments in New Harmony. He found his own thought so mirrored in Robert Owen's writings that he studied them thoroughly, used them to sharpen his own position, and titled one of his books *The New Being*.[64] He also chose "Estranged and Reunited: The New Being" as the subject of his sermon in New Harmony's Roofless Church on the Day of Pentecost, June 2, 1963, when he attended the dedication of a park in his honor. Paul Tillich Park, where his sayings are inscribed on stones to commemorate his life and link to New Harmony's heritage, was created by Jane Blaffer Owen, the town's patron and Tillich's former student at Union Theological Seminary. This shaded grove, where Tillich's ashes were interred after his death in 1965, offers peace and solace to those who walk its pleasant paths.[65] (See color plates, pp. 106–109.)

The evolution of Owen's "new-formed man" never proceeded because the New Moral World experiment on the Wabash would collapse in 1827. None of the structure for the Village of Unity and Mutual Cooperation ever rose from the waiting bricks. A disappointed Thomas Pears later asked, "Where have the square palaces been built . . . ? Where are the gardens?"[66] None of the nearly thirty other Owenite-type communities came even this close to beginning the grandiose quadrangle with its illusory promise of realizing Owen's utopian dream.

If the Owenites did not build their utopian town, totally abandon private property, or revolutionize human nature, they did start enough progressive enterprises in education, science, and communal living to contribute to American cultural, social, and economic development. They also raised a memorial to Owen, his utopian colleague William Maclure, and Maclure's educational protégée Marie Fretageot. Owen knew that recruiting educators, scientists, and cultured individuals was crucial to executing his utopian plan. From December 1825 to January 1826, he and Maclure brought Philadelphia's most accomplished natural scientists, its finest educators, including Fretageot, and several of its other well-to-do residents on a memorable journey to New Harmony. At Pittsburgh, these thirty-five passengers, including Owen's oldest son, Robert Dale Owen, boarded a keelboat, eighty-five feet long by fourteen feet wide, for a cold and accident-prone voyage on the Ohio and Wabash Rivers. Since the depth of the Ohio was temporarily too low for the comfortable steamboat Maclure had intended, the primitive and hurriedly built keelboat had to do. It had four compartments: one for the crew, one for the gentlemen, one for the

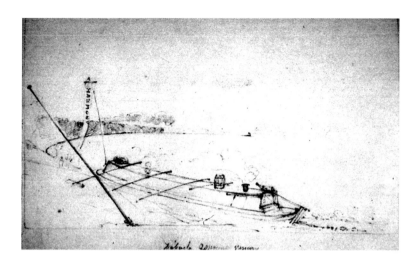

Boatload of Knowledge flying its "Harmony" flag as it landed at Mount Vernon, Indiana, January 23, 1826. Sketch by Charles-Alexandre Lesueur.

Courtesy of the American Philosophical Society.

children, which the adults nicknamed "Purgatory," and another for the women, which the men called "Paradise." The craft itself was christened the *Philanthropist* in honor of Maclure, who financed the trip. Its name was proudly displayed on the side, and atop the vessel flew a flag announcing "Harmony" as its destination.

When the sophisticated voyagers' craft went aground on a sandbar near Father Rapp's Economy, strapping young Harmonist men courageously waded into the cold Ohio to rescue them. After an evening of warm hospitality and a night of free lodging, they were sent on their way refreshed. However, they soon were stranded by river ice that forced them to stay for a month at Safe Harbor, near Beaver, Pennsylvania.[67] Fortunately for Robert Owen, he had left the group at Economy to travel faster overland. He arrived in New Harmony in time to announce in his first speech there, on January 12, 1826, that those about to arrive on the *Philanthropist*

Gerard Troost, c. 1823–1824. Portrait by Charles Willson Peale.

The Academy of Natural Sciences, Ewell Sale Stewart Library and the Albert M. Greenfield Digital Imaging Center for Collections.

Charles-Alexandre Lesueur. Portrait by Charles Willson Peale.

The Academy of Natural Sciences, Ewell Sale Stewart Library and the Albert M. Greenfield Digital Imaging Center for Collections.

represented "more *learning* than ever was before contained in a boat," not "Latin and Greek & other languages but real substantial knowledge."[68] From that day to this, it has been known as the "Boatload of Knowledge."[69] According to Owenite historian Arthur Bestor Jr., the voyage was "in truth one of the significant intellectual migrations of history. It represented the transfer to New Harmony—farther west than any existing American college—of a group of educational and scientific enterprises that had been notable features of the cultural life of Philadelphia."[70]

Along with the geologist, mineralogist, and chemist Gerard Troost, who preceded them, and America's first Pestalozzian teachers, Joseph and Eloisa Neef, who followed them, the boatloaders

Thomas Say. Portrait by Charles Willson Peale.

The Academy of Natural Sciences, Ewell Sale Stewart Library and the Albert M. Greenfield Digital Imaging Center for Collections.

made frontier New Harmony a scientific and educational center for decades. William Maclure had become America's premier geologist after he published a map and explanation of his extensive explorations in 1809.[71] As a social reformer, he believed that all societies could be divided into two classes, productive laborers and nonproductive rulers. Knowledge, he thought, separated the two since knowledge led to wealth and wealth to power and property for a few. To equalize power and property, he advocated setting working people free through ready access to the knowledge that progressive schools and free public libraries could provide. Therefore, using his own business fortune, he attempted to empower the working classes by establishing Pestalozzian and trade schools and working men's libraries.[72] At New Harmony, he also inspired several, including two of the Owen brothers, David Dale and Richard, to become geologists.

Charles-Alexandre Lesueur, also a boatloader, was curator of the Academy of Natural Sciences of Philadelphia. Like the other natural scientists, he welcomed an opportunity to live and teach in New Harmony surrounded by untouched wilderness that offered a ready laboratory for research in his fields of interest: ichthyology, archaeology, and paleontology. As one of America's finest artists, Lesueur drew twelve hundred sketches to document the *Philanthropist*'s voyage and thousands more of the specimens he found and identified on the frontier.[73] Thomas Say was a founder of the Academy of the Natural Sciences of Philadelphia, curator of the American Philosophical Society, and teacher of natural history at the University of Pennsylvania. His research at New Harmony gained him a national reputation in entomology and conchology. His *American Conchology,* published there in 1830, contained beautiful colored plates of shells gathered nearby and painstakingly drawn by his wife, Lucy Sistare Say, who as a young student had also traveled on the *Philanthropist.*[74]

Marie Duclos Fretageot and another experienced Pestalozzian educator, William S. Phiquepal, were also on board. Both taught in Maclure's schools in Paris and Philadelphia before joining the utopian venture. Another passenger was Stedman Whitwell, the English architect. Once in New Harmony, he indulged his interests in meteorology and geography. His weather observations, as printed in the *New-Harmony Gazette,* are perhaps the earliest systematic record of climatic patterns in Indiana and might be instructive in the present age of global warming. Concerned by the repetition of place-names in America and elsewhere, Whitwell invented a system for giving every site on earth its own distinctive name and identifying its location by latitude and longitude. The April 12, 1826, issue of the *Gazette* carried his table of vowels and consonants to substitute for the degrees of latitude and longitude, as follows:

	1	2	3	4	5	6	7	8	9	0
Vowel Substitutes	a	e	i	o	u	y	ee	ei	ie	ou
Consonant Substitutes	b	d	f	k	l	m	n	p	r	t

The English settlers on the eastern edge of New Harmony during one of the town's reorganizations used Whitwell's method to name their section Feiba Peveli. If his scheme had prevailed, New Harmony would have been rechristened Ipba Venul; Pittsburgh, Otfu Veitoup; and Paris, Oput Tedou.[75]

Owen's first speech in New Harmony also indicated that the boatload included "some of the ablest instructors of youth that c[oul]d be found in the U.S. or perhaps in the world." William Pelham enthusiastically wrote his son: "In [New] Harmony there will be the best Library & the best School in the United States."[76] An infant school, higher school, and School of Industry, complemented by lectures, libraries, and museums for adults, came close to proving him right. Owen appointed Maclure to organize and direct this unprecedented educational program. Maclure chose the Neefs, Fretageot, and Phiquepal to supervise the three schools. Thomas Say directed the system during Maclure's long absences.[77] Maclure left permanently in 1827 as the socialistic arrangements collapsed; Marie Fretageot wisely managed Maclure's educational enterprises in New Harmony long after the community experi-

Madame Marie Duclos Fretageot.

Courtesy of the New Harmony Working Men's Institute.

ment ended. She was guided by Maclure's letters, mostly from Europe and Mexico, until her own departure in 1831.[78]

With but two exceptions, the Owenites preferred to convert existing Harmonist structures for their educational and other public purposes rather than to undertake new construction. In 1826, they built a commissary and the No. 1 School House for teaching and boarding students in the higher school. After 1828, this school-house was used for lectures and a ballroom, but neither building exists today. Owen, Maclure, Say, and other community scientists lived in the privileged quarters of Father Rapp's mansion, next to which Say's gravesite and marker can still be seen. (See color plate, p. 185.) The mansion grounds made a special contribution to New Harmony's heritage when Maclure sent Golden Raintree seeds from Mexico to his friend Thomas Say to be planted at the gates. Ever since, the town has been graced with spring showers of golden blooms that spread along its streets.[79] (See color plate, p. 119.) In 1844, the mansion burned. Reconstructed in the late 1840s on the original stone foundation, it was renovated in 1988 as the Rapp-Maclure-Owen House by Kenneth Dale Owen, Robert Owen's great-great-grandson.

New Harmony's infant school in Community House No. 2 replicated Owen's in New Lanark. Begun in 1826, it predated the kindergarten movement in America by decades; the first private kindergarten opened at Watertown, Wisconsin, in 1856 and the first publicly funded one started at St. Louis in 1873.[80] (See color plates, pp. 183–84.) As a boarding school, it housed more than one hundred children ages two through five and was largely intended to shield them from the negative Old Immoral World influence of their parents and families. Mrs. Sarah Cox Thrall later remembered that while in this school "I saw my father and mother twice in two years."[81] Combining Owenite and Pestalozzian methods, Marie Fretageot and Eloisa Neef taught their young charges to share communally, live humanely, and think freely.[82] Mrs. Thrall also recalled, "We went to bed at sundown in little bunks suspended in rows by cords from the ceiling. Sometimes one of the children at the end of the row would swing back her cradle, and, when it collided on the return bound with the next bunk, it set the whole row bumping together. This was a favorite diversion, and caused

Joseph Neef. Portrait by David Dale Owen.

Courtesy of the New Harmony Working Men's Institute.

the teachers much distress."[83] The children often sang a song they made up:

> Number 2 pigs locked up in a pen,
> When they get out, it's now and then
> When they get out, they sneak about
> For fear old Neef will find them out.[84]

The higher school, for six- to twelve-year-olds, reflected Owen's Institution for the Formation of Character and, even more, Maclure's conviction that children should be given mostly practical rather than classical instruction or indoctrination. Maclure once wrote that his own classical education had left him "ignorant as a pig of anything useful."[85] Therefore, classes concentrated on mathematics, science, mechanics, language, writing, art, music, and gymnastics. All teaching focused on direct student involvement, "examining objects in substance or accurate representations of them in designs or prints; anatomy by skeletons and wax figures; geography by globes and maps—most of the last by their own construction," according to Maclure.[86] Sarah Thrall recalled that "there were blackboards covering one side of the schoolroom, and that we had wires, with balls on them, by which we learned to count. We also had singing exercises by which we familiarized ourselves with lessons in various branches."[87] All the scientists gave classroom instruction as well as public lectures for adults on mineralogy, chemistry, zoology, and natural history.

Joseph Neef was the higher school principal and his children, Victor and Louisa, teachers. He had learned his methods directly from Pestalozzi in Switzerland, where he became an instructor. In 1808, he published the first work on educational methods in English printed in America.[88] He still carried a metal ball in his head from fighting as an officer in Napoleon's army and insisted that the boys engage in military drills and that both girls and boys march from place to place in military fashion, often with him joyously in the lead.[89] For all his rough exterior and gruff speech, sometimes punctuated with an oath, Neef was a kindly man who, true to Pestalozzian principles, distained corporal punishment for even the most unruly students.[90] Becoming the students' favorite teacher, he "played, exercised, walked, bathed [swam], threw stones with the pupils all in a childish spirit."[91]

Neef had introduced Maclure to the Pestalozzian system while teaching in Paris. The businessman, who was rapidly becoming a social reformer, became so interested in the potential of these progressive methods for improving the condition of the working classes that he visited Pestalozzi's school in Yverdon, Switzerland, six times after 1805. He established Pestalozzian-type schools in Paris and Spain. Dreaming of an entire American public educational system based on Pestalozzian principles, he invited Pestalozzi to the United States to begin the process. When the aging educator graciously declined, Maclure underwrote the migration of the Neef family to begin the first school of this type in America,

near Philadelphia, in 1809.[92] In March 1826, Maclure brought all four members of the Neef family to New Harmony to teach in the schools. He also advertised the higher and industrial schools in Benjamin Silliman's *American Journal of Science and Arts* and attracted students from as far away as New York and Philadelphia.

All the Pestalozzian teachers must have realized how effective their instruction was from the response and achievements of their students. Neef prided himself on getting students to be skeptical and creative freethinkers, "to gather knowledge by their own senses, to consult experience in every instance, to analyze, to examine, to investigate every thing, to believe nothing."[93] James Miles Wattles, precocious son of Judge James O. Wattles, who was a member of New Harmony's governing committee, studied with Neef, then with Lesueur and Troost in the School of Industry. He examined and questioned the workings of the camera obscura, a small box that had two pinholes and was equipped with lenses that directed images onto a glass screen. In 1828, with advice and light-sensitive chemicals from Gerard Troost, Wattles made an emulsion that fixed an image of the Rappite granary on the screen, which some consider the first photograph made in America.[94] The progressive Pestalozzian system so effectively employed in Maclure's and Owen's schools drew on universal principles for discovering secrets of life and the universe. What better proof of this than the results of Albert Einstein's introduction to Pestalozzian methods? During his year at the public school in Aarau, Switzerland, young Einstein was encouraged to use intuition, conceptual thinking, and visual imagery, and it was there that he carried out the first of his famous visualized thought experiments (*Gedankenexperiment*)—what it would be like to ride alongside a light beam—that led to his revolutionary relativity theory.[95]

The School of Industry introduced the trade school to the United States.[96] With classes in the Harmonist frame church, this school implemented Maclure's idea that each child should learn a useful trade of his or her own choosing. In an arrangement that was similar to the Harmony Society's apprenticeships, more than eighty students from the higher school, nearly all boys, gained occupational skills. William Phiquepal taught printing in Community House No. 2. John Beal, a fellow boatloader, taught carpentry, having constructed his own house using the age-old English "wattle and daub" technique of interweaving small strips of wood set into a mortise-and-tenon wood frame. (See color plate, p. 98.) His house now stands on Church Street. Other craftsmen gave instruction in everything from wood turning, blacksmithing, shoemaking, and hatmaking to taxidermy, joining, wheelwrighting, and farming. Although the community paid lip service to gender equality, girls studied only the traditional homemaking arts of sewing, cooking, dressmaking, and millinery as taught by the women of New Harmony. Maclure intended to pay for all the town's educational programs with the sale of products from his industrial school plus the $100 annual fees of students from outside. Although this goal was never reached, the higher school and the School of Industry did fulfill his dream of linking teaching to research and publication. New Harmony students, perhaps like no others in early America, studied with working scholars whose groundbreaking research they helped to publish as the curriculum focused increasingly on drawing, engraving, and printing. By 1840, when the School of Industry closed, they had helped make thirteen hundred copper plates and had printed works by Owenite and other scientists in the vanguard of ichthyology, conchology, and geology.[97] They also assisted in the publication of Maclure's periodicals: *The Disseminator of Useful Knowledge,* with its banner proclaiming "Ignorance is the fruitful cause of Human Misery," from 1828 to 1841; and *Opinions on Various Subjects* from 1831 to 1838.[98]

Adult education held an important place in Owen's Institution for the Formation of Character in New Lanark and in Maclure's

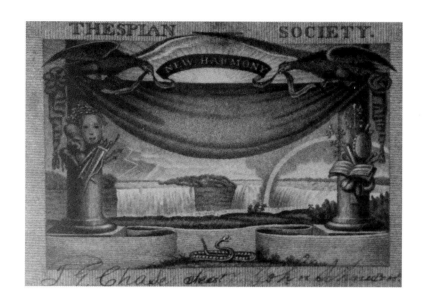

Thespian Society theater ticket, by Charles-Alexandre Lesueur.

Courtesy of the New Harmony Working Men's Institute.

hope to raise the prospects of the working class. The adult school, directed by William Phiquepal, was created for this purpose and conducted in the Rappite brick church, which was renamed the Hall of New Harmony. Eighty students over the age of twelve enrolled for evening classes. Mathematics, science, and useful arts were taught by experts of a caliber scarcely available even in major cities of the East. Gerard Troost lectured on chemistry, Thomas Say on natural history, and Phiquepal on experimental farming. Lesueur taught drawing and painting.[99] Victor Duclos, one of the students, remembered that Lesueur and Say "spent most of their leisure in the woods or in the river searching for shells and catching fish which they painted and described."[100]

The hall also became the scene for various public occasions, enlightening and entertaining the adults with lectures, concerts,

Frances Golden of New Harmony's Golden Family Troupe and founder of the Evansville Civic Theater.

From the Collection of the Indiana State Museum and Historic Sites.

Harmonist Community House No. 4 converted into Thrall's Opera House after 1888. Don Blair Collection.

Courtesy of Special Collections, University of Southern Indiana.

dances, and theatrical performances.[101] William Owen organized the Thespian Society in 1827, which converted the south wing into a theater. Lesueur frescoed and painted the walls with Swiss scenes for the performance of *William Tell*, and his artwork remained there until the building was torn down in 1874.[102] Richard Owen recalled with obvious pleasure having played a role in this very play as "one of the number who would not take off his cap," adding, "My brother William's wife, then Mary Bolton, was Tell's son Albert; she was in boy's clothing, and she played it well."[103] In 1856, the Thespian Society purchased Harmonist Community House No. 4 on Church Street and remodeled it for plays and public use as the Union Hall. When professional actors Martin and Emma ("Bella") Golden moved their family to New Harmony in 1865, New Harmony's national reputation for theater and opera grew with the

Goldens' local and nationwide performances. Known after 1867 as the Golden Troupe, this family won acclaim across the country. One daughter, Grace, became a prima donna of the Castle Square Opera Company in New York City. Another, Frances, founded the Civic Theater in Evansville, which celebrated its eighty-fifth anniversary during its 2010–2011 season.

In 1888, Eugene Thrall added the present façade to the Union Hall, and the building saw its greatest theatrical use from then until 1913 as Thrall's Opera House.[104] Restored by 1969, the Opera House lives on as a historic multipurpose facility. (See color plates, pp. 142 and 178.) Murphy Auditorium became home to theater in New Harmony when it was completed in 1914. (See color plate, p. 182.) Now under the auspices of the University of Southern

Dr. Edward Murphy.

*Courtesy of the New
Harmony Working
Men's Institute.*

Murphy Auditorium with the Working Men's Institute to
the west, both built with funds provided by Dr. Edward
Murphy. Photo, 1925. Don Blair Collection.

Courtesy of Special Collections, University of Southern Indiana.

Indiana's New Harmony Theater, this venue brings the Owenite theatrical and educational heritage full circle. Murphy Auditorium and the modern building for the Workingmen's Institute were gifts from Dr. Edward Murphy, the grateful New Harmony physician who received his early education in the Owen community, where he arrived as an orphan.[105]

Ironically, despite all the benefits of the Owen-Maclure educational system in New Harmony, controversy over the nature of instruction helped destroy the community.[106] Owen, who emphasized broad Pestalozzian objectives in New Lanark, now, like Father Rapp and all radical reformers, demanded that indoctrination in the principles of his ideal system take precedence. The desired formation of superior character had to be hastened from infants to adults. In the infant and higher schools, this implied uniformity imposed on a passive child within a controlled communal setting. Maclure stressed involving children in the learning process and developing their critical intelligence in a freer environment compatible with society at large. With Maclure in charge of New

Harmony's schools, the program naturally emphasized his, rather than Owen's, philosophy of education and social reform. Owen ultimately preferred jeopardizing his own socialistic experiment to compromising with Maclure on their educational differences.[107]

Bitterness over both educational and economic arrangements marked the deteriorating relationship between Owen and Maclure. As early as August 1826, Owen peevishly and publicly blamed Maclure at a town meeting for the fact that their experiment had failed to combine its disparate members into a harmonious community.[108] He charged that Maclure had not given the children of all parents equal access to all the educators and had defeated the communitarian goals by granting children a creative role in classes rather than immersing them in the concepts of the New Moral

World. Education, which Owen had praised as the centerpiece of New Harmony in his first speech to the residents in 1826, became his main excuse for explaining its collapse in his last address on May 6, 1827. He laid all the problems at the feet of Maclure and the teachers he had earlier praised. To Owen's mind, "if the schools had been in full operation, upon the very superior plan which I had been led to expect, so as to convince the parents . . . of the benefits which their children would immediately derive from the system, it would have been, I think, practicable . . . to have succeeded in amalgamating the whole into a Community."[109]

THE OWENITES AFTER NEW HARMONY (1828–1858)

In reality, New Harmony's school system and the libraries created from William Maclure's interest in making knowledge accessible to men who worked with their hands became the longest-lasting social institutions created by the Owen-Maclure community. As a forerunner of Andrew Carnegie, Maclure funded 160 workingmen's libraries, 144 in Indiana and 16 in Illinois. These libraries received $500 each from assets set aside in his will for this purpose.[110] The New Harmony Workingmen's Institute, which he helped form in 1838, became the model for those founded after his death in 1840. This is the only one of the 160 to survive to the present and is a living link to the historic utopian community, a treasure trove of Owenite archival material, and Indiana's oldest functioning library. (See color plates, pp. 113 and 170.) Taken together, the Maclure libraries stimulated the intellectual development of Indiana and southern Illinois, provided the basic collections for later libraries, and initiated the tradition of a free public library system.[111] Furthermore, the statewide system of tuition-free public schools mandated in Indiana's second constitution in 1851 bore the imprint of Maclure and Owen's concerns for an educated public. Robert Dale Owen, deeply affected by his New Harmony experience as

Working Men's Institute, founded in 1838 with funds from William Maclure. It is Indiana's oldest functioning library and a living link to New Harmony's utopian heritage. Don Blair Collection.

Courtesy of Special Collections, University of Southern Indiana.

a young man, insisted upon this provision as a framer of the new constitution and subsequently helped initiate it as a state legislator.

The scientific emphasis which Maclure, Say, Lesueur, and others brought to New Harmony made the village a focus of research in the natural sciences both while the Owen community existed and for decades thereafter. Geology, for which Maclure was then the most noted authority in America, became the chief focus. Gerard Troost both taught geology and carried on exploration. Owen's sons David Dale and Richard were immediately attracted to this exciting field when they arrived in 1828. Geological research was in the first stages of challenging the older religious and scientific concepts about the age of the earth and of revealing the subsurface resources that promised the dawning of the

Robert Dale Owen. Portrait attributed to David Dale Owen.

Courtesy of the New Harmony Working Men's Institute.

industrial age in the United States. In 1837, David Dale Owen conducted the first state-commissioned geological survey of Indiana and was commissioned as a geologist by the federal government, making New Harmony the base for regional surveys from 1837 to 1856, long before the organization of the United States Geological Survey in 1876.[112] During that time, David Dale led one geological expedition that surveyed the present lands of Iowa, Wisconsin, Minnesota, and northern Illinois to identify valuable mineral deposits before the government sold any public lands. The geological training and work of David Dale, his brother Richard, and others attracted to Maclure's hub in New Harmony opened the Midwest to industrialization.

David Dale Owen served as state geologist for Kentucky, Arkansas, and Indiana. Richard Owen succeeded his brother in Indiana. After serving as a colonel in the Civil War, he became a professor of natural science at Indiana University (1864–1879), where a statue honoring his kind treatment of Confederate prisoners at Fort Morton still stands. Appointed Purdue University's first president, he resigned before classes met to continue teaching at Indiana University. Several students in David Dale Owen's geology classes in New Harmony also became state geologists. After 1843, he used the five-story Harmonist granary for his laboratory and museum. Fire reduced this building to three stories in 1878.[113] In 1999, it was adaptively restored as a grand venue for public and private occasions and became known as the Rapp Granary–David Dale Owen Laboratory. (See color plates, pp. 110–111.)

The importance of these research facilities and their use for public instruction was not lost on Robert Dale Owen. As a member of the U.S. House of Representatives, he worked diligently to achieve the congressional action in 1846 that established the Smithsonian Institution in Washington, D.C., as a free national museum, an educational facility to benefit the entire American public. Robert Dale and his brother David Dale submitted a design for its first building and helped select James Renwick Jr. as the architect.[114] This first Smithsonian building came to be known as the Castle. In March 2009, the national and regional contribution of the Owen family was recognized with a special occasion in this venerable building.[115] The Owen brothers' preference for the architecture of the Scottish castles they knew from childhood surfaced again in 1859 when, just a year before his death, David Dale Owen

David Dale Owen.

From the Collection of the Indiana State Museum and Historic Sites.

Richard Owen.

From the Collection of the Indiana State Museum and Historic Sites.

built his fourth geological laboratory adjacent to the granary. It was a "small but sturdy castle in the Scots baronial style, with a tower, turrets, arches, and a lantern window."[116] Above the main entrance he placed an image cast in iron of a trilobite, a specimen he discovered in the Northwest and named in his honor *Isotelus iowensis* Owen. The large Paleozoic fossil fish, sea fan, and blastoid he created for the weathervane continue to celebrate David Dale's beloved geology and to make his lab a prominent feature of the New Harmony skyline.[117] (See color plate, p. 134.)

New Harmony itself became a monument to its founders as the first socialistic community in America. Robert Owen was an early "socialist," a term coined and printed by London Owenites in 1827. In 1837, they first used "socialism" to describe the humanitarian "Social System" he proposed.[118] Owen's benevolent "communal socialism" is not to be confused with the later violent "revolution-

ary socialism" of Karl Marx and Frederick Engels. It is important to set the record straight. Owen sought to unite all classes through goodwill, cooperation, and a surplus of all the necessities of life provided by science and technology. Marx and Engels condemned Owen and all "utopian socialists" as advocates of snail-paced, impractical solutions to the ills of capitalistic society. Yet their own solution, violent overthrow of those in control of the means of production (the bourgeoisie) by the working classes (the proletariat), led many into dictatorships but never into their ill-defined Marxist utopia called "Communism" with a capital "C."

Despite Owen's own verbal attacks on the evils of private property, he did not convert his socialistic town into Rappite-style communism with a small "c." His plan never suggested that anyone be forced to give up their property rights in the belief that a future time of surplus production would render this a moot question. Neither he nor the wealthy William Maclure found it in their natures to turn over their New Harmony property to the otherwise communitarian citizenry any more than Owen had given his mill town

Frances Wright. Portrait by Henry Inman, 1824.

Collection of the New-York Historical Society 155.263.

to the laborers of New Lanark. Thus, in accord with Owen's earliest community plans in which beneficent industrialists would operate communities for the poor and unemployed, New Harmony might be described best as a philanthropic project of two Scottish businessmen turned social reformers.

The feats and flaws of Owenite New Harmony affected non-sectarian communal utopias ever after. Flaws in the communal fabric plagued New Harmony from beginning to end. For many, it became a symbol for human rights, racial equality, and an end to slavery. But its constitution banned African Americans from membership except as "helpers" and suggested they might be trained to become "associates" in communities in Africa, other countries, or elsewhere in America.[119] William Maclure was a strong anti-slavery advocate. Robert Owen was not. They disagreed about whether slaves should be emancipated in the foreseeable future. Maclure abhorred slavery as "a disgrace to the civilization and knowledge of the day" and based on human greed, cruelty and stupidity. It arose, he said, from "prejudices against color, arising from the false supposition of superiority being in the skin."[120] In his will, Maclure provided funding for a settlement of free blacks on New Harmony land, but it never materialized.[121] Robert Owen was not that progressive. While still at New Lanark, he disagreed with abolitionists. He insisted that slave owners were benevolent because it was obviously in their own self-interest. He thought slaves were more content in their present state than they would be if they were freed only to find, like the restless factory workers of Great Britain and Ireland, that mechanical inventions were replacing manual labor. In his words, "Let not therefore the existing slave population be urged forward beyond the present happy ignorant state in which they are until some wise arrangements between the existing white producers and non-producers shall be adjusted to their future benefits."[122]

Frances Wright, one of the most outspoken women on behalf of emancipation and women's rights in the nineteenth century, found New Harmony a welcome platform for her uncompromising attack on slavery in her Fourth of July address there in 1828.[123] Two years earlier, she had become a pioneer among those who used communal arrangements to free, shelter, and educate thousands of slaves before the Civil War in at least eighteen settlements.[124] Her community of Nashoba, near Memphis, Tennessee, operated from 1826 to 1830 in the cause of freedom and racial equality.[125] New Harmony's liberal reputation was later enhanced by Robert Dale Owen, whose position in Congress gave him leverage in urging President Lincoln to issue his Emancipation Proclamation. In 1862, Robert Dale's letters to Lincoln, Secretary of War Edwin M. Stanton, and Secretary of the Treasury Salmon P. Chase arguing for emancipation as a strategy to end the war were widely circulated in the press.[126]

One of the most remarkable stories to come out of slavery in the Old South has to do with a Mississippi plantation run on Owenite principles. Joseph Davis, a prominent lawyer turned planter, saw potential for profit in using Owen's ideas of benevolent labor management, progressive education, and humanitarian treatment. Knowing that Owen had urged wealthy industrialists to assist the poor by establishing altruistic but profitable communities, he realized that a plantation could be made a community just as much as any company town or utopian village. Having undoubtedly discussed Owen and New Harmony during a chance meeting with Frances Wright in Natchez, Davis visited New Harmony for two weeks in June and July 1826.[127] He was deeply impressed by New Harmony's infant school, Pestalozzian educational program, and vocational training. Whether or not he spoke with Owen directly is not known, but he effectively applied the best of Owen's and Maclure's concepts to the three hundred slaves at Davis Bend, his 5,200-acre estate on the Mississippi River, fifteen miles south of Vicksburg. Always as paternalistic as Owen, Davis nevertheless used good food and housing, encouragement of solid family ties, a measure of self-government, and schooling for literacy, trades, and leadership to increase his own wealth and create unheard-of opportunities for African Americans before and after emancipation. As slaves, Benjamin Thornton Montgomery and his son Isa-

iah became even more deeply immersed in Owenism than Davis himself. Benjamin became the manager and later the owner of Davis's plantation. Isaiah seized the chance to found the railroad-sponsored town of Mound Bayou between Vicksburg and Memphis in 1886. Known as "the Jewel of the Delta" and "a Beacon of Hope," it became an unprecedented center of black capitalism and black freedom, whether or not anyone realized it was also a tribute to New Harmony's utopian leadership.[128]

Owenite New Harmony also became a symbol of gender equality even though women were not in fact equal members. Women found new freedoms but also experienced expanded demands upon their traditional domestic services. All were promised equality of social and civil rights, but life was likely to be best for single young women who came to attend school or to escape conditions back home. New Harmony offered weekly dances and concerts attended by liberal and interesting young men. Hannah Fisher Price, although married, testified that "there are many youth of both sexes that are very happy in the variety of each other."[129] Single women could find menial tasks like milking cows fair trade-offs for such opportunities. Many married women in New Harmony and other Owenite communities, especially those from working-class backgrounds, also may have felt that their lot was bettered by the move although they left little written record. Strong evidence suggests, however, that married women from cultured families in the East and those who accompanied husbands seeking a new start in life often felt betrayed by false promises of equality that brought them mostly demeaning labor.[130] Owen rejected the idea of property in people, including spouses and offspring. Yet the traditional view of gender roles permeated the thinking of New Harmony's male leaders. Domestic-type chores became the exclusive and expected duty of women despite the guarantee of equal rights in New Harmony's reorganization as the Community of Equality in January 1826. Their obligations to their own households stretched

Jane Dale Owen Fauntleroy.

From the Collection of the Indiana State Museum and Historic Sites.

Fauntleroy Home. 1815 Harmonist frame dwelling on West Street where Constance Fauntleroy and other ladies founded the Minerva Society in 1859. Photo, 1939. Don Blair Collection.

Courtesy of Special Collections, University of Southern Indiana.

into tiresome cooking, sewing, and cleaning for the entire village. They were not allowed labor credits at the store for most of these onerous tasks, proof that New Harmony did not rise above the universal discrimination women always have experienced while overburdened with domestic duties.[131] Since one objective of Ow-

en's communal egalitarianism was to have the community assume many of the functions of the home, women also were in jeopardy of losing their one time-honored domestic sphere of influence. These circumstances and the outright rebellion of certain wives suggest that the promise of gender equality was broken.

Yet New Harmony and its Owenites established a solid record in the vanguard of advocating and applying women's rights. Jane Dale Owen was the intellectual equal of her better-known brothers, often correcting their written work, especially David Dale's geological reports. She gave public lectures and conducted classes for young ladies. She married scientist and inventor Robert Henry

Fauntleroy, who came to New Harmony in 1827. After Henry died in 1849, she and her children accompanied Robert Dale Owen to his position as minister from the United States to the Kingdom of the Two Sicilies. In the Fauntleroy house, which still stands on West Street, Jane's daughter Constance honored her mother's cultural influence by founding the Minerva Society in 1859, one of the early women's clubs in the United States with a written constitution.[132] The leading feminist of the day, Frances Wright, found Owen's community a place of like-minded progressives. New Harmony adopted a liberating costume for women. Loose-fitting, ankle-length pantaloons under a knee-length or longer skirt gave increased freedom of movement.[133] This style, with a skirt that was often short enough to show the wearer's pantaloons and give hint of the shape of her legs, drew public criticism then and decades later when it appeared again on Amelia Bloomer and the women of communal Oneida, New York. The *Illinois Gazette,* printed at nearby Shawneetown, suggested that

> In beauty there's something to hide and reveal,
> There's a thing which we decency call;
> The old system ladies display a great deal,
> But the new system ladies—show all.[134]

In the community system, Owen promised personal happiness in which the fear, frustration, and sexual tyranny of women in the private family would cease. The ideal society would provide a wider selection of potential mates, an end to unwanted pregnancies, and divorce for unhappy unions. Owen was involved in the birth control movement in Britain as early as 1823, and his son Robert Dale published in 1830 a pioneering tract in New York titled *Moral Physiology.* An indication of how radical this publication was can be gained by the fact that Edward Truelove stood trial in England in 1878 for reprinting it and served four months in jail.[135] Robert Dale further proved his devotion to the interests of women

Frances Wright, wearing a version of the official liberating costume adopted for women in New Harmony's Community of Equality in 1826.

Source unknown.

when, as a drafter of the 1851 Indiana constitution, he sponsored a provision for property rights for married women. Robert Owen's earlier denunciation of traditional marriage in his New Harmony Fourth of July Address in 1826 and the community's sanction of divorce and remarriage after a sixty-day waiting period elicited heated criticism, including untrue charges of promiscuity. One newspaper wrote that "it would be no breach of charity, to class them all with whores and whoremongers, nor to say that the whole group will constitute one great brothel."[136] This charge was blatantly unfair and untrue since Owen never advocated free love. But the general discontent of women in New Harmony and other liberal communal experiments based on Owen's ideas did result in "the creation of a 'women problem' that consumed the [several] Owenite communities and helped to lead to their early demises."[137]

If, despite the ways in which New Harmony stood for gender equality, discontent among its married women contributed to its downfall, Owen's failures in community building did much more. For all his well-intended utopian dreams, he failed in areas crucial to all long-lasting communal societies. Owen did not effectively unite members in his inspired purpose, clearly define or enforce members' financial commitment, develop a self-sustaining economic base, or institute a stable form of governance. Unlike Rapp, who was virtually always present, Owen, the propagandizer for the New Moral World, never consistently assumed the practical role as on-site manager at New Harmony. He left his son William and others in charge as both he and Maclure traveled nearly as many months as they were in the town during its two and a half years as a planned community. Owen waited for more than a year after purchasing the town before defining the financial obligations of residents beyond his first offer that they could live in the former Harmonist buildings and receive supplies from the community store if they donated their labor. In the meantime, many of those who quickly overflowed the town's dwellings proved to be unskilled or

simply freeloaders. Unlike George Rapp, whose devoted disciples built New Harmony and made it prosper in the wilderness, Owen failed to motivate his diverse followers sufficiently to make the former Harmonist fields and factories profitable despite real efforts on his part. As a medium of exchange, he introduced "labor notes" based on hours worked, an idea he had proposed in his 1820 *Report to the County of Lanark*. This "time money" approach did little to improve production, but it deeply impressed resident Josiah Warren. As an advocate of "mutualism," which earned him the title of "America's First Anarchist," Warren adapted Owen's idea for use as notes of labor exchange value in his "Time Stores" in Cincinnati and in his own communal experiments of Equity and Utopia in Ohio and Modern Times in New York.[138] In reality, Owen's philanthropic underwriting of the New Harmony experiment with his fortune may have done most to kill worker initiative.[139] Workers were not motivated as long as they thought Owen's money, bolstered by Maclure's, would finance the experiment.

Added to these problems, Owen could not solve the riddle of bringing his dissatisfied and unruly residents together. The most radical, led by liberal firebrand Paul Brown, advocated complete communism like that of the Harmonists and the Shakers. In one outburst, Brown denounced Owen's New Harmony economic arrangement as a state of perpetual confusion and agitation with its "selling and buying, taking and re-taking, turning and overturning and re-overturning, bargaining, bartering, scheming, maneuvering."[140] Owen, trying to keep the peace during one particularly abusive debate, stood to plead "Kindness everyone, kindness." His interest in unity and goodwill is illustrated by his attraction to the statement by Nicholas Vansittart: "If we cannot reconcile all opinions, let us endeavour to unite all hearts."[141] Owen selected this for the masthead of the *New-Harmony Gazette* and used it to begin a chapter in his autobiography. He undoubtedly would have been pleased to know that over the years many attributed this

Labor Note or Time Money. Robert Owen introduced labor-time currency at New Harmony in the 1820s. This note, endorsed by Josiah Warren, is from 1843, when New Harmony again briefly tried the system as adapted by Warren in his "Time Stores" in Cincinnati and in his Ohio and New York communities. Source unknown.

Courtesy of Historic New Harmony/University of Southern Indiana.

quotation to him. It is still honorably associated with his name in an inscription on the wall behind the public bench at the corner of Main and Church Streets in New Harmony.

For all his good intentions, the "social father" was unable to "unite all hearts" under a single governing instrument for more than a few months. He advocated communal self-government, but his suspicion of elections and electioneering amounted to an avoidance of the democratic process. The New Harmony community was so egalitarian the residents took part in long, often ugly, public debates that produced seven constitutions—the first of which proved unworkable within two weeks.[142] Organizational structure began hopefully with a Preliminary Society and a Community of Equality but deteriorated into acrimonious divisions. Thereafter, small groups, like Macluria (made up of farmers) and Feiba Peveli (composed of English settlers from Illinois), began splitting off under arrangements to use New Harmony land. In May 1826, the most important splintering occurred when Maclure, who wished

to distance himself from Owen, recommended that separate, co-operating communities be formed based on occupations.[143]

When Owen and Maclure sued each other in May 1827 over debts incurred in their financial partnership, Robert Owen's effort to create a working model of the New Moral World came to an end.[144] By 1830, fourteen of the fifteen other Owenite settlements formed in the 1820s in America and Britain also ended. Many Americans saw these failures, especially that of Owen's own New Harmony, as proof that only highly disciplined sectarian groups like the Shakers and Harmonists could make communalism work. It is true enough that vital lessons from American communal experience evaded Owen's notice despite his long acquaintance with the use of such arrangements by sectarian movements on these shores. Even before coming to America, Owen recognized that the cohesive forces binding the Harmonist and Shaker communities together consisted of radical religious doctrines and peculiar practices that he condemned, such as celibacy. Nonetheless, he overlooked the historical clue regarding the high level of commitment necessary to establish and maintain any voluntary community based on the discipline of sharing goods in common.[145] Sectarian leaders, like George Rapp, could call upon the scriptural example of the early Christians using community of property as described in Acts 2 and 4. They could insist that believers' eternal salvation depended on obedience to their divinely ordained, authoritarian leadership. Owen did not have these advantages. He missed the point that his advocacy of Enlightenment, rationalism, and freedom of thought could militate against a unified community unless members became strongly committed to a larger, well-defined, and well-understood central purpose. In New Harmony, he neither screened the incoming residents nor ensured their commitment to his complicated utopian dream by systematic indoctrination. He placed his faith in a progressive educational program to instruct the rising generation as well as adults in the principles of the New Moral World. He might have been frustrated in Indiana by educational and social plans only partly realized, intentions for economic sharing within the community left mostly undefined, and a grand architectural design for a model town unbuilt. Yet he refused to become a doctrinaire communitarian, keeping his system flexible in order to advance his broader social reform goals. Community building never replaced character formation and the achievement of human happiness as the utopian commitment of the Owenite movement. As founding model communities became important to the Owenites after 1816, these safe havens for character development and standard of living improvement always remained for them means to an end—like legislation, education, science, and technology—not an end in itself.

While Owen spent all but seven months of the two and a half years New Harmony endured as a socialistic experiment preaching his utopian gospel elsewhere, his town suffered rancorous debates. Owenism as a reform movement was far from dead, however. John F. C. Harrison notes, "The Owenites at this stage did not abandon their communitarian goals, but there was, not surprisingly, some disillusionment with the methods which had been employed to realize the new moral world. A fresh approach, using new institutions and agencies, seemed to be called for, and the initiative did not need to be confined to the benevolent Mr. Owen."[146] Owenites' attempts to align themselves with emerging workingmen's organizations after 1829 proved far more successful in Britain than in America. As New Harmony and Nashoba ceased to be centers of communal activity, Robert Dale Owen and Frances Wright moved to New York to carry forward the reform crusade. They converted the *New-Harmony Gazette* into the *Free Enquirer*. They also founded the Hall of Science, in which they lectured for women's rights, secularism, and free public boarding schools under the guardianship of the state.[147] Although the "free enquirers" captured segments of the Working Men's Party of New York on

behalf of their public education scheme, this first working-class political movement in America dissolved after the election of 1830. The American Owenites were left without effective institutions to give them leverage before the economic recession of the 1840s helped produce a general communitarian revival in 1843.[148] In Britain, however, rapidly growing working-class institutions became the new agencies through which Owenism sought its objectives. Showing its customary flexibility, "in its attempt to capture the working-class movement [in Britain] Owenism developed along new lines, adapting itself to the demands and interests of artisan leaders."[149]

In total, Owenism and Owenite influence accounted for twenty-nine communities, most of which were attempted in two waves during the 1820s and 1840s. Nineteen of these were in the United States, one in Canada, and nine in England, Scotland, Ireland, and Wales. They began with New Harmony in 1825 and ended when Josiah Warren closed his Modern Times settlement on Long Island in 1863. Spread over nearly four decades, these communal utopias introduced progressive educational methods and fostered freedom of thought and scientific inquiry. They decried organized religion as superstitious tyranny, dissolved unhappy marriages, and altered family life by infant schooling and communal child care. In varying degrees at different times and places, they set aside private property and discrimination by class, sex, and race. Owen himself gave mixed signals about economic and social equality, never reconciling his own innate paternalism with the ideal of egalitarianism. Beyond benevolent paternalism, education, legislation, and communalism, Owen and his followers alertly responded with new methods and new catchwords as circumstances changed or as the popular imagination became captivated by potent concepts like millennialism and spiritualism. Attempting to build whole communities placed an impossible burden on the movement, but Owenites never risked their prime objective of raising the cultural and living standards of the poor and working classes by a total fixation upon communalism or any other single reform method. Both within their experimental communities and by propaganda, public meetings, workers' organizations, cooperatives, and political activism in society at large, Owenites helped effect progressive reform. In Britain, workers' cooperatives and trade unions originated in Owenite activity. In the United States, tax-supported public schools for both girls and boys, public libraries and museums, women's rights, birth control, liberalization of divorce laws, and freedom for the slaves were all part of the Owenite agenda.

Owen died in his hometown of Newtown, Wales, on November 17, 1858, still insisting "that the character of man, is, without a single exception, always formed for him."[150] That same year, he emphatically reaffirmed that he alone, as a near-messianic figure, had been given both this grand insight and the gifts to bring it to reality: "These combined qualities, so essential for this task, have been given to me,—forced upon me by a creating power, in a manner most mysterious, and to this hour undetected by all the faculties yet given to humanity, except by the visible creation of the universe. Thus gifted, without my knowledge or consent, and therefore without the possibility of individual merit, I continue to use these gifts, as I am impelled to do, with the view to change falsehood into truth, and evil into good."[151] Like Rapp, who still believed on the day of his death that Christ would return in his lifetime, Owen in the last year of his life still thought that he had been selected to proclaim the one Great Truth of Character Formation that would usher in the New Moral World.

Ten years later, the American Harriet Martineau wrote that "his peculiar faculties so far fell in with the popular need that he effected much for the progress of society, and has been the cause of many things which will never go by his name."[152] Twenty years following Owen's death, Frederick Engels, the Communist critic of Owenite utopian and communitarian socialism as a frustration of the needed revolution of the proletariat, conceded that "all social movements, all real advance made in England in the interests of the working class were associated with Owen's name."[153] Today, with numerous Owenite reforms featured in modern society, Owen and Owenism excite continued interest. Robert Owen associations exist as far distant as Japan. His famous mill town of New Lanark, Scotland, and utopian village of New Harmony, Indiana, flourish as internationally recognized historic restorations with public interpretive programs.

BEYOND SUCCESS AND FAILURE TO LEGACIES AND LESSONS

PERHAPS THE MOST ASKED QUESTION is whether the Harmonists and Owenites succeeded or failed. Until the 1980s, this question was answered mostly by comparing how long each effort lasted as a communal group. Using this score alone, the Harmonists win easily. The Harmony Society was legally in existence for a century, Owenite New Harmony for a mere two and a half years. Only a few of the other almost thirty communities influenced by Owen lasted even that long. Rosabeth Moss Kanter set twenty-five years as the minimum requirement for considering a communal society successful in her 1972 study, *Commitment and Community*.[1] By this standard, out of ninety-one well-known utopian communities founded by movements in the United States between 1780 and 1860, she found only eleven successful ones. All of these were authoritarian religious sects, including the Harmony Society. According to her, only these achieved the "commitment mechanisms" needed to sustain "cohesion, continuance, and control" for that period of time. None of the secular, democratic, egalitarian groups, including the Owenite movement, did so.

Because the longevity yardstick measures only one dimension of the story, in the 1980s I suggested an approach called "developmental communalism."[2] This method of analysis broadens the perspective from the longevity of individual communities to the length and achievements of their founding movements. This permits us to see communalism as a method of organization rather than an end in itself. Developmental communalism focuses on how religious and reform movements begin; why they choose communal living for security, solidarity, and survival; and in what ways they change over time. It permits us to realize that the most vital movements are flexible. They adjust to internal and external challenges and opportunities. Even in community, they do not freeze into tenets of faith, rules and regulations, forms and structures—not even community of goods. Instead, as "developmental communalism" suggests, they may significantly modify or even shed their communal form altogether in order to let their movements adjust and expand. The Owenite movement did this while the Harmonist did not.

From this perspective, Owen and the followers of his humanitarian socialistic philosophy made their greatest contributions toward reform in the decades following their short-lived communal experiments. Their lectures, publications, and activism for social and political change helped shape the modern world of emancipation of slaves, free tax-supported public schools and libraries, trade unions, consumer-producer cooperatives, equal rights for women, and liberalized divorce laws. Not to be confused with the later violent "revolutionary socialism" of Karl Marx and Frederick Engels, Owen's "humanitarian socialism" moved beyond its confined communal stage to improve the lives of millions of working-class families. By contrast, the Harmony Society of George Rapp became fossilized; its members clung to beliefs like millennialism and practices like celibacy that proved to be dead ends. While they were ideal communitarians, obedient to their community of goods and pleasured in the abundance it provided, the Harmonists' movement died with them. Their success for staying in the communal discipline, including their positive influences in the world of politics and business, must not only be fully recognized but also weighed against their failures—failures of the very Christian affection they professed. The bitter result was suspicion, guilt, heartache, and schism. And their denial of procreation could be considered tantamount to generational suicide.

Thus, Harmonist and Owenite New Harmony give us a rare opportunity to derive lessons from two diverse utopian experiments, one religious, the other secular. George Rapp drew on the poignant power of millennialism yet never led his disciples into the kingdom of God on earth. Robert Owen used the enticing promise of early socialism but never delivered his followers into the New Moral World. The Harmonist experience suggests that if we are to address the needs and problems of our own times, we must not sit idly by awaiting divine intervention. The Owenite experience suggests that direct confrontation of social ills may require novel approaches and dogged perseverance to achieve the success that proves the strength of humanitarianism. The troublesome internal conflicts experienced by each group illustrate the vital importance of balancing unity and diversity to attain harmony and sustain longevity—for movements, nations, or humanity. The Rappites and Owenites endured sufficient oppression under the prophetic dominance of Father Rapp and the aristocratic paternalism of Robert Owen to remind us to reject authoritarianism whether it claims religious or secular authority. And finally, the flaws in Harmonist pacifism and Owenite egalitarianism help us realize the importance of the nonviolent resolution of conflict, especially in an age of uncivil public discourse, religious intolerance, and nuclear weapons.

In all, the two New Harmony experiments bequeath to us an invaluable utopian heritage. This heritage, according to Robert Dale Owen, is "an example" to strive for all that is desirable and "a beacon" to beware of all that is destructive.[3] From the Golden Rose to the Golden Raintree, New Harmony is a place of hope, peace, and beauty. Here all can dream of, believe in, and work toward a better "destiny of man" in a "new moral world."

NOW

Along the Wabash River

Canoe event on the Wabash River

Granary Street gate

Atheneum

Atheneum

David Lenz House garden

David Lenz House interior

Orpheus Fountain of the Cathedral Labyrinth

Cathedral Labyrinth

Orpheus Fountain at Cathedral Labyrinth

West Street cabins

No. 5

Macluria double log cabin

Rope making at West Street cabin

John Beal House on Church Street showing English-style wattle-and-daub building technique

Carol's Garden on North Street

Carol's Garden on North Street

Ceremonial gates of Roofless Church

GALLERY

Roofless Church

Roofless Church

Roofless Church

Overlook in Roofless Church

Tillich Park

NOW

Bust of Paul Tillich by James Rosati

Commemorative stone to
Paul Tillich in Tillich Park

Stone with Paul Tillich quotation in Tillich Park

Rapp Granary–David Dale Owen Laboratory on Granary Street

Interior of the upper floor of the Rapp Granary–David Dale Owen Laboratory on Granary Street

Rapp Granary–David Dale Owen Laboratory on Granary Street

Working Men's Institute

Harmonist fire engine, the "Pat Lyon," in the Working Men's Institute museum

Ribeyre Gymnasium

Harmony Society
sundial on Community
House No. 2

The Poet's House on Granary Street

"Dutch biscuit" construction in Harmonist Community House No. 2 on Main Street

Golden Raintree

Sign on Church Street, recognizing New Harmony's beautiful trees and its use of nonpolluting golf carts for local transportation

Church Street Victorians

Victorian downtown on Church Street

Town Hall on Church Street

Main Cafe

Outside dining at the Red Geranium Restaurant

Relaxing scene at Old Rooming House on Church Street

Golden Raintree blossoms

Reconstructed Harmonist Labyrinth on Main Street

NOW

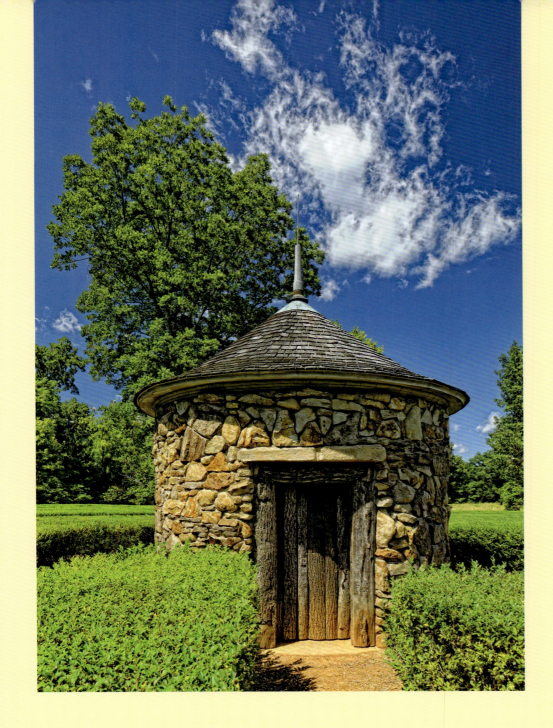

Temple in the center of the reconstructed
Harmonist Labyrinth on Main Street

The text visible on the ceiling dome reads (arranged radially):

A harmonious and united society of men may be ... to be ...

Again a day is passed and a step made nearer the end. Our time runs away ... the joys ... which is lofty.

The day of our Lord is drawing near and will dominate over all that is high and humiliate all which is lofty.

The Golden treasure of this world to those who know how to preserve it, is Friendship.

The Creator of the Universe has always in view the happiness of all the human race.

God requires no more of any human being than one man of honor and reputation requires of another.

Under the serene sky and friendly clime the fruits of noble achievement and wholesome constitutions come to greater maturity.

We endure and suffer, labor and toil, sow and reap, with and for each other.

Temple ceiling in the reconstructed Harmonist Labyrinth on Main Street

1830 Owen House

1830 Owen House on Tavern Street

David Dale Owen House and fourth laboratory on Church Street

Fossil weather vane on David Dale Owen's fourth geological laboratory on Church Street. From top: Paleozoic fish, screw-shaped bryozoan (sea fan) named Archimedes, and echinoderm, known as a blastoid.

NOW

The New Harmony Inn

Jane Blaffer Owen, 1915–2010

Footbridge behind New Harmony Inn

*Saint Francis and the Birds by Frederick
Franck at New Harmony Inn*

Original Harmony Society cabin, now part of the Barrett Gate House on North Street

Roman numeral V. A Harmonist standardized construction timber marking on an original Harmonist cabin, now part of the Barrett Gate House on North Street.

GALLERY

Solomon Wolfe House on Granary Street

Harmonist kitchen house

Thrall's Opera House

The French Spy at Thrall's Opera House

Plein Air Paint Out on Granary Street

Kunstfest

145

Church and Main Streets during Kunstfest

Annual Antiques Show

Fourth of July at the Maclure Park Bandstand

Fourth of July Golf Cart Parade

Fourth of July

Antique Tractor Show on Granary Street

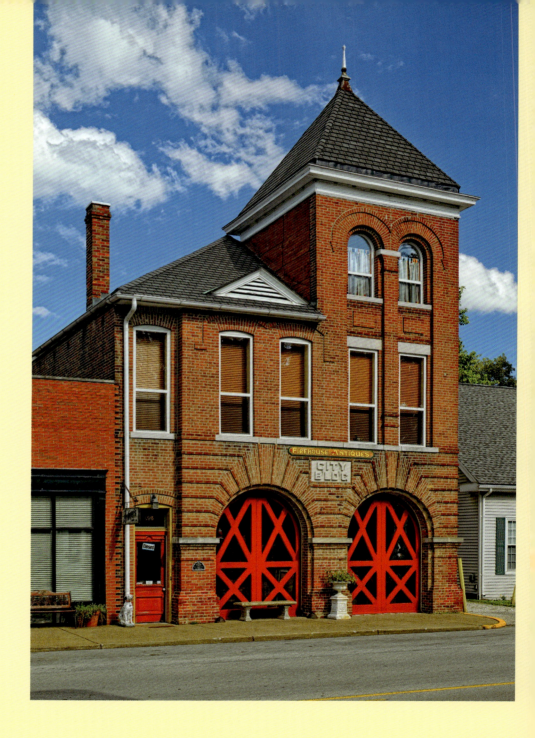

Original New Harmony firehouse

A labyrinth of golden leaves in the Harmonist Cemetery

Harmonist Cemetery with Atheneum

David Lenz House on North Street

Original Harmony Society cabin, now part of the Barrett Gate House on North Street

Harmony Society hop house on North Street

Granary Street

Harmony Society kitchen next to Harmonist Community House No. 2 on Main Street

An interpreter as Harmonist prophet
George Rapp in Church Park

Church Park, with replica of the Harmonist Door of Promise

Fretageot House

Golden Raintree at the Keppler House on Tavern Street

Victorian house on Tavern Street

Saint Stephen's Episcopal Church

GALLERY

Saint Stephen's Episcopal Church

Bagpiper leading a procession on North Street

Chapel at New Harmony Inn Entry House

New Harmony Inn Entry House Chapel

Working Men's Institute library

Robert Owen purchasing New Harmony from Father George Rapp. 1908 painting in the Working Men's Institute.

A. C. Thomas House on West Street

Red Bud Park on Church Street

GALLERY

Warhol at New Harmony Gallery of Contemporary Art

Victorian downtown, Main Street

Victorian downtown, Main Street

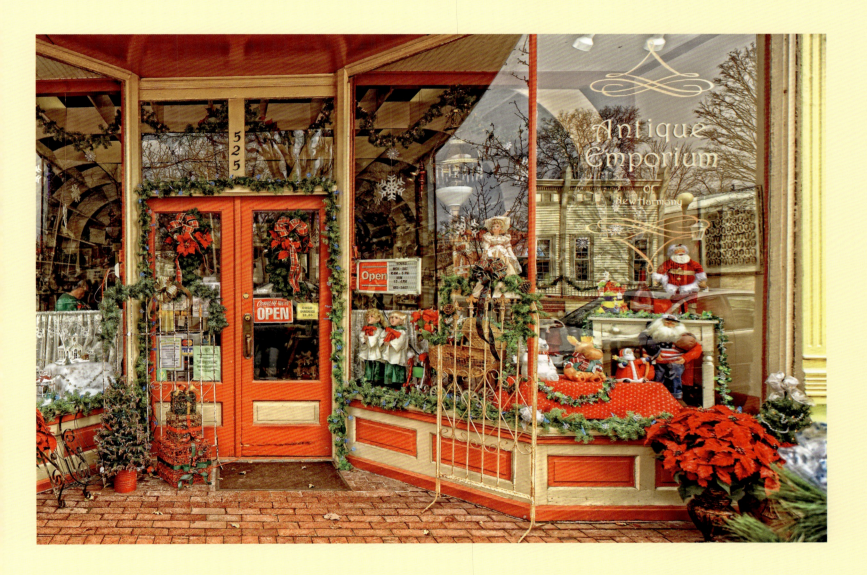

Victorian downtown, Church Street

Holiday ball at Thrall's Opera House

West Street cabins

West Street cabins

Roofless Church

Murphy Auditorium

Harmonist Community House No. 2 on Main Street, the location of the Owenite infant school—the first in the United States

Harmonist Community House No. 2 from Church Street

Thomas Say Tomb on Main Street with the rebuilt and adaptively restored Rapp-Maclure-Owen House in the background. It was known in the Harmonist and Owenite communities as No. 5.

Victorian Main Street

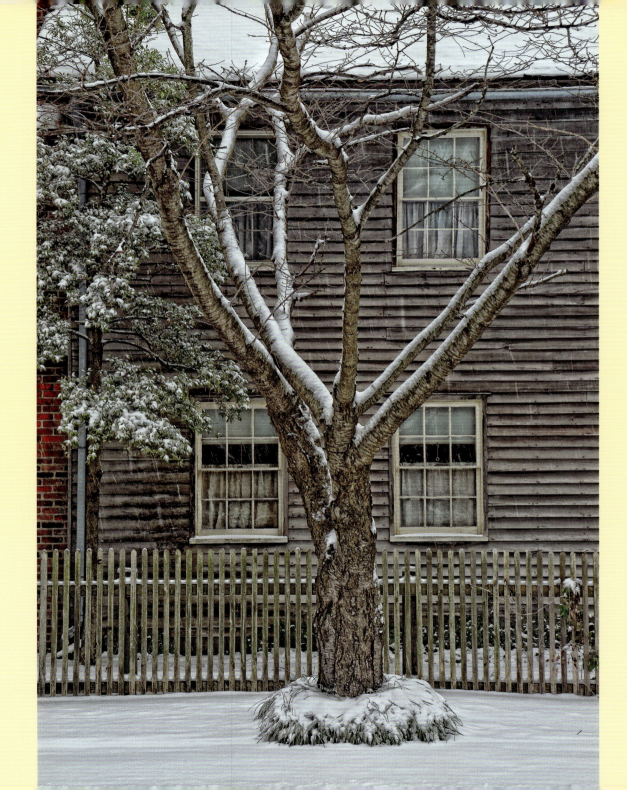

Harmonist house on Granary Street

GALLERY

Owen Community House

NOW

Owen Community House

Orchard House on North Street

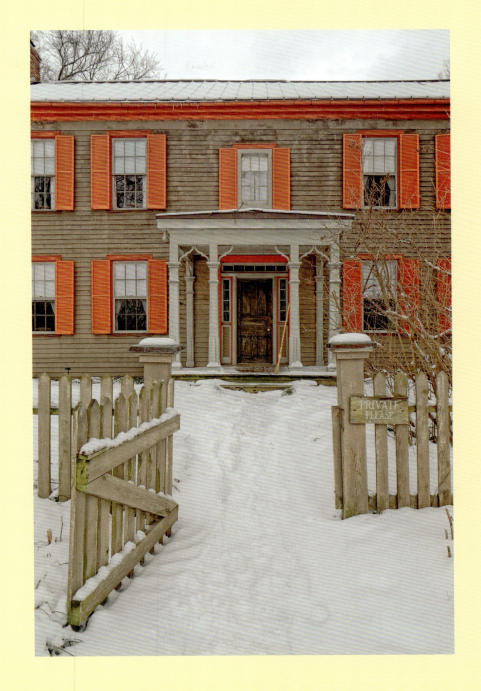

Orchard House

NOTES

1. THE HARMONISTS

1. Unless specifically noted, the history of the Harmony Society is based on Karl John Richard Arndt, *George Rapp's Harmony Society, 1785–1847*, rev. ed. (Rutherford, N.J.: Fairleigh Dickinson University Press, 1972); Arndt, *George Rapp's Successors and Material Heirs, 1847–1916* (Rutherford, N.J.: Fairleigh Dickinson University Press, 1971); Arndt, *George Rapp's Disciples, Pioneers and Heirs: A Register of the Harmonists in America* (Evansville: University of Southern Indiana Press, 1994); Arndt's eight documentary histories of the Harmony Society published by the Harmony Society Press, Indiana Historical Society, and Peter Lang, Inc.; Donald E. Pitzer, ed., *America's Communal Utopias* (Chapel Hill: University of North Carolina Press, 1997), 57–87; and Anne Taylor, *Visions of Harmony: A Study in Nineteenth-Century Millenarianism* (New York: Oxford University Press, 1987).

2. Arndt, *George Rapp's Harmony Society*, 492.

3. Taylor, *Visions of Harmony*, 10.

4. Arndt, *George Rapp's Harmony Society*, 458.

5. Karl J. R. Arndt, *Harmony on the Connoquenessing: George Rapp's First American Harmony, 1803–1815* (Worcester, Mass.: Harmony Society Press, 1980), 160.

6. Arndt, *George Rapp's Harmony Society*, 15.

7. Arndt, *Harmony on the Connoquenessing*, 227–28.

8. Ibid., 138.

9. Karl John Richard Arndt, *The Indiana Decade of George Rapp's Harmony Society: 1814–1824* (Worcester, Mass.: American Antiquarian Society, 1971), 23; Arndt, *George Rapp's Harmony Society*, 255–56. Karl Arndt traced the earliest use of "Harmonie" in German literature to 1669 when the communal, pietistic "Hungarian Anabaptists," now known as the Hutterites, were called a "Harmonia." Akin to the Harmonists in all but celibacy and the emphasis on Sunwoman, the eight hundred Hutterites who emigrated from Russia to the Dakotas in the 1870s were assisted by the Harmony Society.

10. [George Rapp], *Thoughts on the Destiny of Man, particularly with reference to the present times* ([New Harmony]: The Harmony Society in Indiana, 1824), 88.

11. Ibid., 72–73.

12. Ibid., 73.

13. Ibid.

14. Arndt, *George Rapp's Disciples*, 16; Arndt, *George Rapp's Harmony Society*, 72–76.

15. Arndt, *Harmony on the Connoquenessing*, 80–91, 253.

16. Arndt, *George Rapp's Harmony Society*, 72 ff.

17. Arndt, *Harmony on the Connoquenessing*, 80.

18. Ibid., 137–38.

19. Paul Douglas, *Architecture, Artifacts, and Arts in the Harmony Society of George Rapp: The Material Culture of a Nineteenth-Century American Utopian Community* (Lewiston, N.Y.: Edwin Mellen Press, 2008), 106–109.

20. Taylor, *Visions of Harmony*, 21; Richard D. Wetzel, *Frontier Musicians on the Connoquenessing, Wabash, and Ohio: A History of the Music and Musicians of George Rapp's Harmony Society, 1805–1906*, (Athens: Ohio University Press, 1976).

21. Douglas, *Architecture*, 85, 151–53, 172.

22. Quoted in Arndt, *Harmony on the Connoquenessing*, 270; Arndt, *George Rapp's Harmony Society*, 97.

23. [Rapp], *Thoughts*, 32.

24. Arndt, *Harmony on the Connoquenessing*, 225.

25. Karl J. R. Arndt, *George Rapp's Separatists, 1700–1803: The German Prelude to Rapp's American Harmony Society* (Worcester, Mass.: Harmonie Society Press, 1980), 280–81; Eileen Aiken English, *Demographic Directory of the Harmony Society* (Clinton, N.Y.: Richard Couper Press, 2011), 106.

26. *The Diaries of Donald Macdonald, 1824–1826*, with an introduction by Caroline Dale Snedeker, Indiana Historical Society Publications, vol. 14, no. 2 (Indianapolis: Indiana Historical Society, 1942), 247; Arndt, *George Rapp's Harmony Society*, 252, 554.

27. Arndt, *George Rapp's Harmony Society*, 379–99.

28. John W. Larner Jr., "'Nails and Sundrie Medicines': Town Planning and Public Health in the Harmony Society, 1805–1840," *Western Pennsylvania Historical Magazine* 45 (June 1962): 119; Donald E. Pitzer and Josephine M. Elliott, "New Harmony's First Utopians, 1814–1824," *Indiana Magazine of History* 75 (September 1979): 235; Arndt, *Indiana Decade*, 19.

29. Karl J. R. Arndt, *A Documentary History of the Indiana Decade of the Harmony Society, 1814–1824*, vol. 1, *1814–1819* (Indianapolis: Indiana Historical Society, 1975), 8.

30. Ibid., 6, 745.

31. Quoted in Arndt, *Indiana Decade*, 13.

32. Ibid., 14.

33. Arndt, *Documentary History of the Indiana Decade*, vol. 1, 25–26; Arndt, *George Rapp's Successors*, p. 109, indicates that 100 died at Harmony, 230 at New Harmony, and 379 at Economy to 1874.

34. Paul H. Douglas, "The Material Culture of the Harmony Society," *Pennsylvania Folklore* 24 (Spring 1975): 6; Arndt, *Documentary History of the Indiana Decade*, vol. 1, 71.

35. Arndt, *George Rapp's Harmony Society*, 146.

36. Ibid., 176. The street names are written on a town map drawn later from memory by Harmonist Eusebius Böhm and included in a cover pocket in Karl J. R. Arndt, *Harmony on the Wabash in Transition: George Rapp to Robert Owen, 1824–1828* (Worcester, Mass.: Harmony Society Press, 1982).

37. Arndt, *George Rapp's Harmony Society*, 176, 277.

38. Weingartner's 1832 map is inserted in Karl J. R. Arndt, *A Documentary History of the Harmony Society, 1814–1824*, vol. 1, *1814–1819* (Indianapolis: Indiana Historical Society, 1975).

39. Arndt, *George Rapp's Harmony Society*, 274.

40. Quoted in Arndt, *Indiana Decade*, 7.

41. Ibid.

42. Ibid.

43. Pitzer and Elliott, "New Harmony's First Utopians," 263.

44. Arndt, *Indiana Decade*, 9.

45. Pitzer and Elliott, "New Harmony's First Utopians," 263.

46. Quoted from Elias Pym Fordham, *Personal Narrative of Travels in Virginia, Maryland, Pennsylvania, Ohio, Indiana and Kentucky: And of a Residence in the Illinois Territory: 1817–1818*, ed. Frederic Austin Ogg (Cleveland: Arthur H. Clark, 1906), in Arndt, *George Rapp's Harmony Society*, 176.

47. Arndt, *George Rapp's Harmony Society*, 215.

48. Ibid., 119.

49. Quoted in ibid., 242–43.

50. Ibid., 205.

51. See the Weingartner and Böhm maps cited above.

52. Arndt, *George Rapp's Harmony Society*, 276.

53. Ibid., 174–76.

54. Ibid., 176.

55. Ibid., 205; Douglas Wissing, "Indiana's First Brewers: The Germans at New Harmony," *Traces of Indiana and Midwestern History* 22, no. 2 (Spring 2010): 42–45.

56. Arndt, *Indiana Decade*, 18.

57. Quoted in Wissing, "Indiana's First Brewers," 43–44.

58. "Indiana's First Beer," *Traces of Indiana and Midwestern History* 22, no. 2 (Spring 2010): 46–47.

59. English, *Demographic Directory of the Harmony Society*, 96–97, 229–30, 232, 249, 259.

60. Ibid., 48, 229–30, 232, 249.

61. Arndt, *George Rapp's Harmony Society*, 210.

62. Arndt, *Documentary History of the Indiana Decade*, vol. 1, 80.

63. Arndt, *Indiana Decade*, 5.

64. Christiana F. Knoedler, *The Harmony Society: A Nineteenth Century American Utopia* (New York: Vantage, 1954), 97.

65. Donald E. Pitzer, "Education in Utopia: The New Harmony Experience," in *Indiana Historical Society Lectures, 1976–1977: The History of Education in the Middle West* (Indianapolis: Indiana Historical Society, 1978), 76.

66. [Rapp], *Thoughts*, 75–76.

67. Pitzer and Elliott, "New Harmony's First Utopians," 244, 247, 270–71.

68. [Rapp], *Thoughts*, 69.

69. Pitzer, "Education in Utopia," 86, 88–89.

70. Wetzel, *Frontier Musicians*, 111.

71. Ibid., 21–25, 32, 145.

72. Wetzel, *Frontier Musicians*, 30–34, 140–43; Pitzer, "Education in Utopia," 86–89.

73. Pitzer and Elliott, "New Harmony's First Utopians," 238.

74. Arndt, *George Rapp's Harmony Society*, 319.

75. George B. Lockwood, *The New Harmony Movement* (New York: D. Appleton and Company, 1905), 26.

76. Quoted in Lorna Lutes Sylvester, ed., "Miner K. Kellogg: Recollections of New Harmony," *Indiana Magazine of History* 64 (March 1968): 55.

77. Pitzer and Elliott, "New Harmony's First Utopians," 248.

78. Snedeker, *Diaries of Donald Macdonald*, 249.

79. Quoted in Arndt, *George Rapp's Harmony Society*, 276–77.

80. Quoted in Arndt, *Documentary History of the Indiana Decade*, vol. 1, 799.

81. Quoted in ibid., 390.

82. Quoted in ibid., 176.

83. Quoted in ibid., 270.

84. William Hebert, "From a Visit to the Colony of Harmony in Indiana [1825]," in *Indiana as Seen by Early Travelers*, vol. 3, ed. Harlow Lindley (Indianapolis: Indiana Historical Collections, 1916), 334.

85. Ibid.

86. Arndt, *George Rapp's Harmony Society*, 276.

87. Lockwood, *New Harmony Movement*, 36; Arndt, *George Rapp's Successors*, 106–108.

88. Karl J. R. Arndt, "George Rapp's Harmony Society," in *America's Communal Utopias*, ed. Donald E. Pitzer (Chapel Hill: University of North Carolina Press, 1997), 61.

89. Arndt, *Indiana Decade*, 14; Arndt, *George Rapp's Harmony Society*, 96–97, 158, 163, 215, 235, 240, 243, 247–48, 251–52; Karl J. R. Arndt, "The Strange and Wonderful New World of George Rapp and His Harmony Society," *Western Pennsylvania Historical Magazine* 57 (April 1974): 161.

90. John R. Yeatts, *Revelation* (Scottdale, Pa.: Herald Press, 2003), 391–95.

91. Arndt, *George Rapp's Harmony Society*, 459.

92. Ibid., 255–57; Arndt, *Indiana Decade*, 23.

93. [Rapp], *Thoughts*, 53.

94. Ibid., 46–47, 53, 64–65.

95. Ibid., 66.

96. Arndt, *Indiana Decade*, 18–23.

97. Ibid., 18.

98. Ibid., 19.

99. Karl J. R. Arndt, *A Documentary History of the Indiana Decade of the Harmony Society*, vol. 2, *1820–1824* (Indianapolis: Indiana Historical Society, 1978), 9–13.

100. Arndt, *Indiana Decade*, 18.

101. Pitzer and Elliott, "New Harmony's First Utopians," 231.

102. Arndt, *George Rapp's Successors*, 86.

103. Arndt, *Indiana Decade*, 18–19.

104. Arndt, *George Rapp's Successors*, 85–86.

105. Arndt, *Indiana Decade*, 18; Arndt, *George Rapp's Harmony Society*, 177.

106. Arndt, *Indiana Decade*, 19.

107. Arndt, *George Rapp's Harmony Society*, 260–65.

108. Ibid., 157.

109. Ibid., 176.

110. Arndt, *George Rapp's Harmony Society*, 262; Arndt, *Documentary History of the Indiana Decade*, vol. 1, 78, 216–17, 440–43.

111. Arndt, *Documentary History of the Indiana Decade*, vol. 2, 9–13.

112. Diary of George Rapp, May 4, 1823, quoted in Arndt, *George Rapp's Harmony Society*, 248.

113. These names are seen on the town maps drawn from memory by Harmonists Wallrath Weingartner and Eusebius Böhm as inserts in Arndt, *Documentary History of the Indiana Decade of the Harmony Society*, vol. 1, and Arndt, *Harmony on the Wabash*.

114. Quoted in Henry H. Snelling, *The History and Practice of the Art of Photography* (New York: G. P. Putnam, 1849), 12.

115. Lockwood, *New Harmony Movement*, opposite page 36.

116. Interview in New Harmony on April 23, 2010, with Dr. Ruth Reichmann, program director, Max Kade German-American Center, Indianapolis, Indiana.

117. Interview in New Harmony on May 1, 2010, with Dr. David L. Rice, president emeritus, University of Southern Indiana, and overseer for the reconstruction of the Rapp Granary–David Dale Owen Laboratory.

118. Arndt, *George Rapp's Harmony Society*, 178–79; John D. Barnhart and Donald F. Carmony, *Indiana: From Frontier to Industrial Commonwealth*, vol. 1 (New York: Lewis Historical Publishing, 1954), 300–13; Arndt, *Indiana Decade*, 19.

119. Arndt, *Indiana Decade*, 15–17.

120. Arndt, *George Rapp's Harmony Society*, 189, 638n3 for ch. 16.

121. The fame of the Harmony Society is also reflected in Goethe's *Wilhelm Meister's Wanderjahre* and the poetry of the Hungarian Nikolaus Lenau, who may have lived with the Harmony Society briefly when in America in 1832 and 1833. Arndt, *Indiana Decade*, 12.

122. Arndt, *George Rapp's Harmony Society*, 260.

123. Ibid., 189.

124. Eileen Aiken English, Sarah Buffington, and Eric Castle, "Out of Harmony: Secession from the Harmony Society," Exhibit script, Old Economy Village, Ambridge, Pa., 2008, 5–7.

125. Arndt, *George Rapp's Harmony Society*, 353.

126. Rapp was also aware of the Moravian communal arrangement called the "General Economy." Whether this affected his use of the term "divine Economy" is a matter of speculation. See Wetzel, *Frontier Musicians*, 140.

127. [Rapp], *Thoughts*, 63–65.

128. Arndt, *George Rapp's Harmony Society*, 269–71.

129. Arndt, *Indiana Decade*, 19.

130. English, et al., "Out of Harmony," 10. Both *The Seer of Prevorst* (*Die Seherin von Prevorst*), about Hauffe's visions, and the Berlenburg Bible

(*Berleberger Bibel*) influenced Rapp's decision to predict Christ's coming.

131. English, et al., "Out of Harmony," 11.

132. Ibid., 14.

133. Arndt, *George Rapp's Descendants, Pioneers, and Heirs,* 23.

134. Arndt, "George Rapp's Harmony Society," in *America's Communal Utopias,* ed. Donald E. Pitzer (Chapel Hill: University of North Carolina Press, 1997), 77–78.

135. Ibid., 78.

136. Pitzer, *American Communal Utopias,* 88–134, 159–80, 279–96.

137. Arndt, *George Rapp's Successors,* 121–22, 129–38.

138. Ibid., 124–29.

139. Quoted in Arndt, *George Rapp's Harmony Society,* 599.

140. Arndt, *George Rapp's Successors,* 61–84.

141. Arndt, *Indiana Decade,* 25.

2. THE OWENITES

This history of Owenism includes excerpts from *America's Communal Utopias,* edited by Donald E. Pitzer. Copyright © 1997 by the University of North Carolina Press. Used by permission of the publisher.

1. The best summary of Owen's views is his Robert Owen, *The Book of the New Moral World* (London: The Home Colonization Society, 1836–1844). This was reprinted in 1970 by Augustus M. Kelley, Publishers, Clinton, N.Y. It also appears as vol. 3 of the first comprehensive edition of all Owen's major writings, *The Works of Robert Owen,* ed. Gregory Claeys, 4 vols. (London: Pickering and Chatto, 1993).

2. Robert Owen, *The Life of Robert Owen. Written by Himself. With Selections From His Writings & Correspondence,* 2 vols. (London: Effingham Wilson, 1857–1858; reprint, Clinton, N.Y.: Augus-

tus M. Kelley, Publishers, 1967). See also Frank Podmore, *Robert Owen: A Biography* (London: George Allen & Unwin, 1906); G. D. H. Cole, *The Life of Robert Owen,* 2nd ed. (New York: Macmillan, 1930), and Margaret Cole, *Robert Owen of New Lanark, 1771–1858* (London: Batchworth Press, 1953).

3. John F. C. Harrison, *Quest for the New Moral World: Robert Owen and the Owenites in Britain and America* (New York: Scribner's, 1969), 52.

4. Ibid., 159.

5. Ian Donnachie and George Hewitt, *Historic New Lanark: The Dale and Owen Industrial Community since 1785* (Edinburgh: Edinburgh University Press, 1993). The "silent monitor" is pictured in Donald Carmony and Josephine M. Elliott, "New Harmony, Indiana: Robert Owen's Seedbed for Utopia," *Indiana Magazine of History* 76 (September 1980): 192.

6. Donnachie and Hewitt, *Historic New Lanark,* 97–107.

7. Arthur Bestor Jr., *Backwoods Utopias: The Sectarian Origins and the Owenite Phase of Communitarian Socialism in America, 1663–1829* (Philadelphia: University of Pennsylvania Press, 2nd enl. ed., 1970), 64–66.

8. Robert Owen *Report to the County of Lanark* (May 1, 1820), reprinted in Owen, *Life of Robert Owen,* vol. 1A, 302.

9. Bestor, *Backwoods Utopias,* 64–66.

10. Robert Owen, *Book of the New Moral World,* 6th part, 85; Paul K. Conkin, *Tomorrow a New World: The New Deal Community Program* (Ithaca, N.Y.: Cornell University Press, 1959).

11. Owen, *Life of Robert Owen,* vol. 1A, following title page.

12. Owen, *Life of Robert Owen,* vol. 1, 184–85.

13. Arndt, *Indiana Decade,* 16–17.

14. Donnachie and Hewitt, *Historic New Lanark,* 71; Harrison, *Quest for the New Moral World,* 37, 41, 49, 50, 63, 68, 75, 76, 135; Taylor, *Visions of Harmony,* 65, 66.

15. Robert Owen, "Fourth Letter," September 6, 1817, reprinted in Owen, *Life of Robert Owen,* vol. 1A, 119, 120.

16. Bestor, *Backwoods Utopias,* 67.

17. John F. C. Harrison, "Robert Owen's Quest for the New Moral World in America," and Robert G. Clouse, "Robert Owen and the Millennialist Tradition," in *Robert Owen's American Legacy,* ed. Donald E. Pitzer (Indianapolis: Indiana Historical Society, 1972), 33, 42–55.

18. Robert Owen, "Oration, Containing a Declaration of Mental Independence," *New-Harmony Gazette* (July 12, 1826), reprinted in Donald E. Pitzer and Josephine M. Elliott, *New Harmony's Fourth of July Tradition* (New Harmony, Ind.: Raintree Books, 1976), 9–13.

19. Owen, *Book of the New Moral World,* 4th part, 1.

20. Owen, *Book of the New Moral World,* 1st part, 69–70; 4th part, 1–62.

21. Taylor, *Visions of Harmony,* 64; Harrison, *Quest for the New Moral World,* 4, 64, 78–85.

22. Quoted in Taylor, *Visions of Harmony,* 65.

23. Harrison, *Quest for the New Moral World,* 80; Merle Curti, "Robert Owen in American Thought," *Robert Owen's American Legacy: Proceedings of the Robert Owen Bicentennial Conference,* ed. Donald E. Pitzer (Indianapolis: Indiana Historical Society, 1972), 56–67.

24. Robert Owen and Robert Dale Owen, eds., *The Crisis* (London, 1833), title page.

25. Robert Owen, *New View of Society,* 16.

26. Robert Dale Owen, preface to *Outline of the System of Education at New Lanark* (Glasgow: n.p., 1824), reprinted in *Owenism & the Working Class: 1821–1834,* in the series *British Labour*

Struggles before 1850 (Salem, N.H.: Ayer Company Publishers, 1972).

27. *A Brief Sketch of the Religious Society of People Called Shakers,* 1817, reprinted in Robert Owen, *Life of Robert Owen,* vol. 1A, 145–54; Harrison, *Quest for the New Moral World,* 99, 100.

28. George Flower, *History of the English Settlement in Edwards County, Illinois, founded in 1817 and 1818 by Morris Birkbeck and George Flower,* ed. E. B. Washburne, (Chicago, 1882), 372–73; Harrison, *Quest for the New Moral World,* 53–54; Arndt, *Indiana Decade,* 20–21.

29. Bestor, *Backwoods Utopias,* 102–103; Donnachie and Hewitt, *Historic New Lanark,* 135–36; Harrison, *Quest for the New Moral World,* 163; Taylor, *Visions of Harmony,* 74–75.

30. Snedeker, *Diaries of Donald Macdonald,* 186–91, 228–32.

31. Joel W. Hiatt, ed., *Diary of William Owen from November 10, 1824, to April 20, 1825* (Indianapolis, Ind.: Bobbs-Merrill Company, 1906; reprint, Clinton, N.Y.: Augustus M. Kelley, Publishers, 1973), 53.

32. Josephine Mirabella Elliott, ed., *Partnership for Posterity: The Correspondence of William Maclure and Marie Duclos Fretageot, 1820–1833* (Indianapolis: Indiana Historical Society, 1994), 290.

33. Bestor, *Backwoods Utopias,* 102–103.

34. Taylor, *Visions of Harmony,* 160–61.

35. Robert Owen to William Allen, April 21, 1825, "Owen Papers," Manchester Co-operative Union, Manchester, England, quoted in Harrison, *Quest for the New Moral World,* 55.

36. "Address on Wednesday, the 27th April, 1825, in the Hall of New-Harmony," *New-Harmony Gazette,* vol. 1 (October 1, 1825).

37. William Maclure to Marie Fretageot, Louisville, Ky., September 25, 1826, quoted in Arthur Bestor, ed., *Education and Reform at New Harmony,* Indiana Historical Society Publications, vol. 15 (Indianapolis: Indiana Historical Society, 1948), 371.

38. Robert Owen, *Robert Owen's Opening Speech, etc.* (Cincinnati: Published for Robert Owen, 1929), title page; Earl Irvin West, "Early Cincinnati's 'Unprecedented Spectacle,'" *Ohio History* 79 (Winter 1970): 4–17.

39. For Alexander Campbell's version of the debate, see Robert Richardson, *Memoirs of Alexander Campbell* (1897; Germantown, Tenn.: Religious Book Service, n.d.), 263–84.

40. All thirty Owenite-type communities are listed in "Appendix: America's Communal Utopias Founded by 1965," *America's Communal Utopias,* ed. Pitzer, 481–82.

41. Harrison, *Quest for the New Moral World,* 195.

42. A dozen new Owenite-type communities were founded during this time. See "Appendix," *America's Communal Utopias,* ed. Pitzer, 481–82.

43. Harrison, *Quest for the New Moral World,* 87.

44. Bestor, *Backwoods Utopias,* 104–109.

45. Ibid., 95–98.

46. Ibid., 100, 108, 153–58; Carl J. Guarneri, "Brook Farm and the Fourierist Phalanxes," and Robert P. Sutton, "An American Elysium: The Icarian Communities," in *America's Communal Utopias,* ed. Pitzer, 159–80, 279–96.

47. Lucy Jayne Botscharow, "Disharmony in Utopia: Social Categories in Robert Owen's New Harmony," *Communal Societies* 9 (1989): 76–90.

48. Paul Brown, *Twelve Months in New Harmony* (Cincinnati, 1827; reprint, Philadelphia: Porcupine Press, 1972).

49. Thomas Clinton Pears, ed., *New Harmony: An Adventure in Happiness, Papers of Thomas and Sarah Pears,* Indiana Historical Society Publications, vol. 11 (Indianapolis: Indiana Historical Society, 1933), 60.

50. Karl Bernhard, "Travels through North America, during the Years 1825 and 1826," in *Indiana as Seen by Early Travelers,* ed. Harlow Lindley, vol. 3 (Indianapolis: Indiana Historical Collections, 1916), 431.

51. Botscharow, "Disharmony in Utopia," 89, 90.

52. The dress style is pictured in Elliott, *Partnership for Posterity,* 352, 455, 584.

53. Carmony and Elliott, "New Harmony, Indiana," 261.

54. Owen's model village is pictured in ibid., 200–202. Owen placed a drawing of it in his *New View of Society* (London, 1817). See also Stedman Whitwell's *Description of an Architectural Model from a design by Stedman Whitwell, Esq. for a Community upon a Principle of United Interests as Advocated by Robert Owen, Esq.* (London: Hurst Chance & Co., 1830); reprinted in *Cooperative Communities: Plans and Descriptions,* Kenneth E. Carpenter, advisory ed. (New York: Arno Press, 1972).

55. Bestor, *Backwoods Utopias,* 129.

56. Bestor, *Backwoods Utopias,* 128–29; Carmony and Elliott, "New Harmony, Indiana," 201.

57. [Sealsfield], *The Americans As They Are* (London, 1828), 66–71, in Lindley, *Early Travelers,* 528.

58. As reported in the Washington *National Intelligencer* (December 6, 1825).

59. "Letters to William Creese Pelham, 1825 and 1826," in Lindley, *Early Travelers,* 365, 376, 394.

60. Carl J. Guarneri, "Brook Farm," in *America's Communal Utopias,* ed. Donald E. Pitzer (Chapel Hill: University of North Carolina Press, 1997), 160.

61. Owen, *Book of the New Moral World,* 1st part, 74–76.

62. *Millennial Gazette,* January 1, 1857, 18.

63. Owen, *Life of Robert Owen*, vol. 1A, 114.

64. Gert Hummel, "Hope for a New World," in *Paul Tillich's Theological Legacy: Spirit and Community*, ed. Frederick J. Parrella (Berlin: Walter de Gruyter & Co., 1995), 15. The essays in this anthology grew out of a meeting of Tillich scholars and theologians in New Harmony in 1993 at the invitation of Jane Blaffer Owen.

65. Ibid., 13–16. Professor Clark Kimberling of the University of Evansville found one quotation in Tillich Park that he felt connected to New Harmony's legacy in several ways. From Tillich's "Man and nature belong together in their created glory—in their tragedy and in their salvation," he took "man" to represent the town's communitarians, "nature" to suggest its naturalists, "tragedy" to touch a universal in New Harmony and all human history, and "salvation" to crown "the human experience as a promise consistent with Harmonist faith and Tillich's mission." See http://faculty.evansville.edu/ck6/bstud/tillich.html.

66. Pears, *Papers of Thomas and Sarah Pears*, 91–93.

67. Robert Dale Owen recorded daily events in his journal, published as *To Holland and to New Harmony: Robert Dale Owen's Travel Journal, 1825–1826*, ed. Josephine M. Elliott, Indiana Historical Society Publications, vol. 23 (Indianapolis: Indiana Historical Society, 1969), 235–64. See also Donald E. Pitzer, "The Original Boatload of Knowledge Down the Ohio River: William Maclure's and Robert Owen's Transfer of Science and Education to the Midwest, 1825–1826," *Ohio Journal of Science* 89 (December 1989): 128–42. On Thomas Say, see Patricia Tyson Stroud, *Thomas Say: New World Naturalist* (Philadelphia: University of Pennsylvania Press, 1992).

68. William Pelham to his son, New Harmony, January 13, 1826, "Pelham Letters," in Lindley, *Early Travelers*, 405.

69. Mrs. Thomas Pears to Mrs. Benjamin Bakewell, New Harmony, March 10, 1826, in Pears, *Papers of Thomas and Sarah Pears*, 71.

70. Bestor, *Backwoods Utopias*, 133–34.

71. William Maclure, "Observations on the Geology of the United States Explanatory of a Map," *Transactions of the American Philosophical Society* 6 (1809): 411–28.

72. Leonard Warren, *Maclure of New Harmony: Scientist, Progressive Educator, Radical Philanthropist* (Bloomington: Indiana University Press, 2009), passim.

73. B. Ritsert Rinsma, *Alexandre Lesueur, Tome I: Un Exploration et Artiste Français au pays de Thomas Jefferson* (Editions du Havre de Grâce, 2007). English trans. Leslie Roberts, *Alexandre Lesueur, Explorer and Artist in the Land of Thomas Jefferson* (pending).

74. Harry B. Weiss and Grace M. Ziegler, *Thomas Say: Early American Naturalist* (Springfield, Ill., 1931); Stroud, *Thomas Say*.

75. William E. Wilson, *The Angel and the Serpent: The Story of New Harmony* (Bloomington: Indiana University Press, 1964), 153–54.

76. William Pelham to his son, February 9, 1826, "Pelham Letters," in Lindley, *Early Travelers*, 411.

77. Stroud, *Thomas Say*.

78. Elliott, *Partnership for Posterity*; Bestor, *Education and Reform*.

79. Don Blair, *The New Harmony Story* (reprint, New Harmony, Ind.: New Harmony Publications Committee, 1993), 60–62

80. George B. Lockwood, *The New Harmony Movement* (New York: D. Appleton and Company, 1905), 287.

81. Lockwood, *New Harmony Movement*, 246; www.watchtownhistory.org.

82. On Owenite and Pestalozzian education see Bestor, *Backwoods Utopias*; Gerald Gutek, *Joseph Neef: The Americanization of Pestalozzianism* (University: University of Alabama Press, 1978); Gerald Gutek, *Pestalozzi and Education* (New York: Random House, 1968); Donald E. Pitzer, "Education in Utopia: The New Harmony Experience," *Lectures, 1976–1977: The History of Education in the Middle West* (Indianapolis: Indiana Historical Society, 1978), 74–101.

83. Pitzer, "Education in Utopia," 74–101.

84. Ibid.

85. Maclure to Benjamin Silliman, October 19, 1822, in George P. Fisher, *Life of Benjamin Silliman*, 2 vols. (New York: Charles Scribner, 1866).

86. Quoted in Gutek, *Joseph Neef*, 46

87. Quoted in Lockwood, *New Harmony Movement*, 246.

88. Joseph Neef, *Sketch of a Plan and Method of Education* (Philadelphia, 1808).

89. Lockwood, *New Harmony Movement*, 246.

90. Ibid., 247–50; Warren, *Maclure of New Harmony*, 85.

91. Warren, *Maclure of New Harmony*, 85.

92. Ibid.

93. Gutek, *Joseph Neef*, 48.

94. "A Moon-Base or The New Atlantis," lecture by Ritsert Rinsma of the University of Le Havre, France, at New Harmony, Indiana, April 9, 2010. Information based on Henry H. Snelling, *The History and Practice of the Art of Photography* (New York: G. P. Putnam, 1849), 9–13.

95. Walter Isaacson, *Einstein: His Life and Universe* (New York: Simon & Schuster, 2007), 25–27.

96. The Rensselaer [Polytechnic] Institute of Troy, New York, opened in 1824, but stressed technology rather than trades.

97. These works included parts of Charles-Alexandre Lesueur's proposed *American Ichthyology*; Thomas Say's *Descriptions of Some New Terrestrial and Fluviatile Shells of North America*, serialized in Maclure's *Disseminator* from 1829 to 1831; Say's

landmark *American Conchology* in seven volumes (1830–1838); and a new edition of Francois Andre Michaux's *North American Silva* that appeared in 1841.

98. Warren, *Maclure of New Harmony*, 232–33.

99. Gutek, *Joseph Neef*, 49.

100. Victor Colin Duclos, "Diary and Recollections," in Lindley, *Early Travelers*, 546.

101. Carmony and Elliott, "New Harmony, Indiana," 212, 214–15, 220.

102. Ibid., 247.

103. Jacob Schneck and Richard Owen, *The History of New Harmony* (Evansville, Ind., 1890), 11.

104. Pitzer and Elliott, "New Harmony's First Utopians," 279; Janet R. Walker, *Wonder Workers on the Wabash* (New Harmony, Ind.: Historic New Harmony, 1999), 49–51; Blair, *New Harmony Story*, 66–67.

105. Carmony and Elliott, "New Harmony, Indiana," 236; Walker, *Wonder Workers*, 54–55; Blair, *New Harmony Story*, 66–67.

106. Charles Burgess, "A House Divided: Robert Owen and William Maclure at New Harmony," *Journal of the Midwest History of Education Society* 3 (1975): 110–21; Paul R. Bernard, "Irreconcilable Opinions: The Social and Educational Theories of Robert Owen and William Maclure," *Journal of the Early Republic* 8 (Spring 1988): 21–44; Pitzer, "Education in Utopia," 93–98.

107. For Maclure's social philosophy and reform theories, see his *Opinions on Various Subjects, Dedicated to the Industrious Producers*, 3 vols. (New Harmony, Ind.: Printed at the School Press, 1831–1838), and the introductions in John S. Doskey, ed., *The European Journals of William Maclure* (Philadelphia: American Philosophical Society, 1988); and Elliott, *Partnership for Posterity*. Also see Maclure's articles in *The Disseminator of Useful Knowledge*, printed in New Harmony after 1828.

108. The best summary of this ending scenario to Owenite New Harmony is in Bestor, *Backwoods Utopias*, 191–201.

109. *New-Harmony Gazette*, May 9, 1827, 54.

110. Elliott, *Partnership for Posterity*, 13, 14, 833; Josephine M. Elliott, "William Maclure: Patron Saint of Indiana Libraries," *Indiana Magazine of History* 94, no. 2 (June 1998): 178–90.

111. Elliott, *Partnership for Posterity*, 13, 14.

112. W. B. Hendrickson, *David Dale Owen: Pioneer Geologist of the Middle West*, vol. 27 (Indianapolis: Indiana Historical Collections, 1943).

113. Pitzer and Elliott, "New Harmony's First Utopians," 276.

114. Warren, *Maclure of New Harmony*, 324n9.

115. "How the Devil It Got There: The Politics of Form and Function in the Smithsonian Institution," lecture by John Sears at the Smithsonian, March 10, 2009, and at New Harmony, Indiana, October 9, 2009.

116. Taylor, *Visions of Harmony*, 224.

117. Historic New Harmony archival file photos of an exhibit in the Keppler House. The other fossil specimens on the weather vane immediately below the Paleozoic fish are a screw-shaped fossil bryozoan (sea fan) named *Archimedes* and a fossil echinoderm, known as a blastoid, belonging to the genus *Pentremites*. The bulbous-shaped middle piece is the living chamber of the lowest fossil, and the segmented stem below it functioned to attach the animal to the sea floor.

118. Arthur E. Bestor Jr., "The Evolution of the Socialist Vocabulary," *Journal of the History of Ideas* 9 (June 1948): 277.

119. Taylor, *Visions of Harmony*, 109.

120. Maclure, *Opinions*, 1:30–31, 42–44; 2:370; 3:109–12, 154–56, 247–49, quoted in Warren, *Maclure of New Harmony*, 201.

121. Warren, *Maclure of New Harmony*, 280; Maclure's will, Fretageot Collection (New Harmo-

ny Working Men's Institute), quoted in Carmony and Elliott, "New Harmony, Indiana," 222.

122. Quoted in Taylor, *Visions of Harmony*, 109–10.

123. *New-Harmony Gazette*, July 9, 1828. See Celia Morris Eckhardt, *Fanny Wright: Rebel in America* (Cambridge, Mass.: Harvard University Press, 1984).

124. Some 3,000 to 5,000 slaves were freed and trained in communal settings in the four decades before the Civil War. See William H. and Jane H. Pease, *Black Utopia: Negro Communal Experiments in America* (Madison: State Historical Society of Wisconsin, 1963), 4.

125. On Nashoba, see Eckhardt, *Fanny Wright*, 89–95, 108–34; Bestor, *Backwoods Utopias*, 49, 114, 218–26.

126. *New York Evening Post*, August 8 and November 22, 1862; *New York Daily Tribune*, October 23, 1862. Robert Dale Owen also published *Emancipation Is Peace* (Loyal Publication Society, New York No. 22, n.d.).

127. Joel Nathan Rosen, *From New Lanark to Mound Bayou: Owenism in the Mississippi Delta* (Durham, N.C.: Carolina Academic Press, 2011), 81–85; Elliott, *Partnership for Posterity*, 382, 408.

128. Rosen, *From New Lanark*, 85–155.

129. Hannah Fisher Price to Joseph Warner, March 10, 1826; Fisher-Warner Papers, Friends Historical Library, Swarthmore College, Swarthmore, Pa.

130. "Voices from New Harmony: The Letters of Hannah Fisher Price and Helen Gregoroffsky Fisher," *Communal Societies* 12 (1992): 113–28. On women in Owenite and other communal societies see "Women's Experiences in the American Owenite Communities," in Wendy Chmielewski et al., eds., *Women in Spiritual and Communitarian Societies in the United States* (Syracuse, N.Y.: Syracuse University Press, 1993), 38–51; Jill Harsin,

"Housework and Utopia: Women and the Owenite Communities," in Ruby Rohrich and Elaine H. Baruch, eds., *Women in Search of Utopia* (New York: Schocken Books, 1984), 76–80; Carol A. Kolmerten's *Women in Utopia: The Ideology of Gender in the American Owenite Communities* (Bloomington: Indiana University Press, 1990).

131. Taylor, *Visions of Harmony*, 109.

132. Carmony and Elliott, "New Harmony, Indiana," 180–81, 198–89, 255–56; Taylor, *Visions of Harmony*, 218–19.

133. See the sketches in Elliott, *Partnership for Posterity*, 455, 584.

134. *Shawnee-Town Illinois Gazette,* July 12, 1826, 330, quoted in Bestor, *Backwoods Utopias,* 222.

135. Harrison, *Quest for the New Moral World,* 61, 62, 253n.

136. *Indiana Journal* (Indianapolis), November 14, 1826, 3; Bestor, *Backwoods Utopias,* 222–23.

137. Kolmerten, *Women in Utopia,* 90; Kolmerten, "Women's Experiences," 39; Kolmerten, "Voices from New Harmony," 114.

138. *New-Harmony Gazette,* October 1, 1825, and February 15, 1826, and Bestor, *Backwoods Utopias,* 184–85. See the analysis of Owenism and New Harmony in Edward K. Spann, *Brotherly Tomorrows: Movements for a Cooperative Society in America, 1820–1920* (New York: Columbia University Press, 1989), 17–49. On Josiah Warren and his "Time Stores," see a poem from the Cincinnati *Saturday Evening Chronicle* reprinted in the *New-Harmony Gazette,* December 26, 1827; Lockwood,

New Harmony Movement, 294–306; William Bailie, *Josiah Warren, the First American Anarchist: A Sociological Study* (Boston: Small, Maynard & Company, 1906); John Humphrey Noyes, *History of American Socialisms* (Philadelphia: Lippincott, 1870), 95–101; and Pitzer, *America's Communal Utopias,* 120, 123, 130n489.

139. Bestor, *Backwoods Utopias,* 180, 181.

140. Brown, *Twelve Months in New Harmony,* 86.

141. Robert Owen, *The Life of Robert Owen,* vol. 1, 272.

142. Elliott, *Partnership for Posterity,* 289.

143. Bestor, *Backwoods Utopias,* 170–201; Carmony and Elliott, "New Harmony, Indiana," 175–76.

144. Bestor, *Backwoods Utopias,* 197, 198; Carmony and Elliott, "Seedbed," 176–79.

145. Religious orders in Europe displayed this. On the importance of commitment mechanisms to sustaining communal groups over time, see Rosabeth Moss Kanter, *Commitment and Community: Communes and Utopias in Sociological Perspective* (Cambridge, Mass.: Harvard University Press, 1972).

146. Harrison, *Quest for the New Moral World,* 195.

147. Bestor, *Backwoods Utopias,* 226; Harrison, *Quest for the New Moral World,* 196.

148. Harrison, *Quest for the New Moral World,* 196. See Brian J. L. Berry, *America's Utopian Experiments: Communal Havens from Long-Wave Crises* (Hanover, N.H.: University Press of New

England, 1992), 22, 58, on the possible effects of economic fluctuations on the formation of Owenite communities.

149. Harrison, *Quest for the New Moral World,* 196.

150. Owen, *A New View of Society,* 3rd essay.

151. "A New Year's Gift to the World, for 1858," in Owen, *The Life of Robert Owen,* vol. 1A, vi.

152. Harriet Martineau, *Biographical Sketches, 1852–1875* (London, 1877), 307.

153. Friedrich Engels, *Anti-Duhring: Herr Eugen Duhring's Revolution in Science* (1878; Chicago: C. H. Kerr & Company, 1935), 296, 297.

3. BEYOND SUCCESS AND FAILURE TO LEGACIES AND LESSONS

1. Rosabeth Moss Kanter, *Commitment and Community: Communes and Utopias in Sociological Perspective* (Cambridge, Mass.: Harvard University Press, 1972).

2. Donald E. Pitzer, "Developmental Communalism: An Alternative Approach to Communal Studies," *Utopian Thought and Communal Experience,* ed. Dennis Hardy and Lorna Davidson (Enfield, England: Middlesex Polytechnic, 1989), 68–76, reprinted in *Community Service Newsletter* 39 (January–April 1991); Donald E. Pitzer, "Response to Lockyer's 'From Developmental Communalism to Transformative Utopianism,'" *Communal Studies* 29, no. 1 (2009): 15–21.

3. *New York Free Enquirer,* June 10, 1829.

BIBLIOGRAPHY

HARMONIST SELECTED BIBLIOGRAPHY

Arndt, Karl John Richard. *A Documentary History of the Indiana Decade of the Harmony Society, 1814–1824.* 2 vols. Indianapolis: Indiana Historical Society, 1975–1978.

———. *Economy on the Ohio, 1826–1834: George Rapp's Third American Harmony.* Worcester, Mass.: Harmony Society Press, 1984.

———. *George Rapp's Disciples, Pioneers, and Heirs: A Register of the Harmonists in America.* Ed. Donald E. Pitzer and Leigh Ann Chamness. Evansville: University of Southern Indiana Press, 1994.

———. *George Rapp's Harmony Society, 1785–1847.* Rev. ed. Rutherford, N.J.: Fairleigh Dickinson University Press, 1972.

———. *George Rapp's Re-established Harmony Society: Letters and Documents of the Baker-Henrici Trusteeship, 1848–1868.* New York: Peter Lang, 1993.

———. *George Rapp's Separatists, 1700–1803: The German Prelude to Rapp's Harmony American Society.* Worcester, Mass.: Harmonie Society Press, 1980.

———. *George Rapp's Successors and Material Heirs, 1847–1916.* Rutherford, N.J.: Fairleigh Dickinson University Press, 1971.

———. *George Rapp's Years of Glory: Economy on the Ohio, 1834–1847.* New York: Peter Lang, 1987.

———. *Harmony on the Connoquenessing, 1803–1815: George Rapp's First American Harmony.* Worcester, Mass.: Harmony Society Press, 1980.

———. *Harmony on the Wabash in Transition to Rapp's Divine Economy on the Ohio and Owen's New Moral World at New Harmony on the Wabash, 1824–1826.* Worcester, Mass.: Harmony Society Press, 1982.

———. *The Indiana Decade of George Rapp's Harmony Society, 1814–1824.* Worcester, Mass.: American Antiquarian Society, 1971.

Douglas, Paul. *Architecture, Artifacts, and Arts in the Harmony Society of George Rapp: The Material Culture of a Nineteenth-Century American Utopian Community.* Lewiston, N.Y.: Edwin Mellen Press, 2008.

English, Eileen Aiken. *Demographic Directory of the Harmony Society.* Clinton, N.Y.: Richard W. Couper Press, 2011.

Knoedler, Christiana F. *The Harmony Society: A Nineteenth Century American Utopia.* New York: Vantage, 1954.

Kring, Hilda A. *The Harmonists: A Folk-Cultural Approach.* Metuchen, N.J.: Scarecrow Press, 1973.

Lockwood, George B. *The New Harmony Movement.* New York: D. Appleton and Company, 1905.

Pitzer, Donald E. "Education in Utopia: The New Harmony Experience." *Indiana Historical Society Lectures, 1976–1977: The History of Education in the Middle West.* Indianapolis: Indiana Historical Society, 1978.

———, ed. *America's Communal Utopias.* Chapel Hill: University of North Carolina Press, 1997.

Pitzer, Donald E., and Josephine M. Elliott. "New Harmony's First Utopians, 1814–1824." *Indiana Magazine of History* 75 (September 1979): 225–300.

[Rapp, George]. *Thoughts on the Destiny of Man, Particularly with reference to the Present Times.* New Harmony: The Harmony Society in Indiana, 1824.

Wetzel, Richard D. *Frontier Musicians on the Connoquenessing, Wabash, and Ohio: A History of the Music and Musicians of George Rapp's Harmony Society, 1805–1906.* Athens: Ohio University Press, 1976.

HARMONIST VISUALS

Finding Harmony: Communal Societies & The Town of New Harmony. DVD. Produced by Ball State University, Muncie, Ind., 2008.

Old Stones in New Harmony. Video. Produced by WNIN, Evansville, Ind., 1999.

OWENITE SELECTED BIBLIOGRAPHY

Bestor, Arthur. *Backwoods Utopias: The Sectarian and Owenite Phases of Communitarian Socialism in America, 1663–1829.* Philadelphia: University of Pennsylvania Press, 1950. Expanded edition, 1970.

Carmony, Donald F., and Josephine M. Elliott. "New Harmony, Indiana: Robert Owen's Seedbed for Utopia." *Indiana Magazine of History* 76 (September 1980): 161–261.

Claeys, Gregory, ed. *The Works of Robert Owen.* London: Pickering and Chatto, 1993.

Cole, G. D. H. *The Life of Robert Owen.* 2nd ed. New York: Macmillan, 1930.

Cole, Margaret. *Robert Owen of New Lanark.* London: Batchworth Press, 1953.

Donnachie, Ian, and George Hewitt. *Historic New Lanark.* Edinburgh: University of Edinburgh Press, 1993.

Eckhardt, Celia. *Frances Wright: Rebel in America.* Cambridge, Mass.: Harvard University Press, 1983.

Elliott, Josephine M. *Partnership for Posterity: The Correspondence of William Maclure and Marie Duclos Fretageot, 1820–1833.* Indianapolis: Indiana Historical Society, 1994.

Gutek, Gerald Lee. *The Americanization of Pestalozzianism.* University: University of Alabama Press, 1978.

Harrison, John F. C. *Quest for the New Moral World: Robert Owen and the Owenites in Britain and America.* New York: Charles Scribner's Sons, 1969.

Kolmerten, Carol A. *Women in Utopia: The Ideology of Gender in the American Owenite Communities.* Bloomington: Indiana University Press, 1990.

Leopold, Richard W. *Robert Dale Owen.* Cambridge, Mass.: Harvard University Press, 1940.

Lockwood, George B. *The New Harmony Movement.* New York: D. Appleton and Company, 1905.

Morton, A. L. *The Life and Ideas of Robert Owen.* New York: International Publishers, 1969.

Owen, Robert. *The Book of the New Moral World.* London: The Home Colonization Society, 1842–1844. Reprint, New York: Augustus M. Kelley, Publishers, 1970.

———. *The Life of Robert Owen. Written By Himself. With Selections from His Writings and Correspondence.* 2 vols. London: Effingham Wilson, 1857–1858. Reprint, New York: Augustus M. Kelley, Publishers, 1967.

Podmore, Frank. *Robert Owen: A Biography.* 2 vols. London: George Allen & Unwin, 1906.

Pitzer, Donald E, ed. *Robert Owen's American Legacy.* Indianapolis: Indiana Historical Society, 1972.

———. "Education in Utopia: The New Harmony Experience." *Indiana Historical Society Lectures, 1976–1977: The History of Education in the Middle West.* Indianapolis: Indiana Historical Society, 1978.

———, ed. *America's Communal Utopias.* Chapel Hill: University of North Carolina Press, 1997.

Rinsma, B. Ritsert. *Alexandre Lesueur, Tome I: Un Exploration et Artiste Français au pays de Thomas Jefferson* (Editions du Havre de Grâce, 2007). English trans. Leslie Roberts, *Alexandre Lesueur, Explorer and Artist in the Land of Thomas Jefferson* (pending).

Taylor, Anne. *Visions of Harmony: A Study in Nineteenth-Century Millenarianism.* New York: Oxford University Press, 1987.

Warren, Leonard. *Maclure of New Harmony: Scientist, Progressive Educator, Radical Philanthropist.* Bloomington: Indiana University Press, 2009.

OWENITE VISUALS

Heaven on Earth: The Rise and Fall of Socialism. PBS Miniseries, June 2005. Video. Produced by New River Media, Washington, D.C.

The New Harmony Experience. DVD. Produced by Historic New Harmony, New Harmony, Ind., 1978.

The Noble Experiment: The Owen Community, 1825–1827. DVD. Produced by Ball State University, Muncie, Ind., 2008.

DONALD E. PITZER is Professor Emeritus of History and Director Emeritus of the Center for Communal Studies at the University of Southern Indiana in Evansville. He is a founder and first president of the Communal Studies Association and International Communal Studies Association. With New Harmony as the springboard for his career in communal history, he has taught, lectured, and published worldwide on the Harmonists, Owenites, other communitarians, and his theory of developmental communalism. He edited and contributed "The New Moral World of Robert Owen and New Harmony" to the anthology *America's Communal Utopias.*

DARRYL D. JONES has exhibited his photographs in New York, in Boston, and throughout the Midwest. In addition, a forty-year retrospective exhibit was held at American University, Cairo, Egypt. Among his books are *Indianapolis, A Simple and Vital Design, The Spirit of the Place, Sweet Owen, Indiana, Indiana II, Destination Indiana, Indiana in Stereo, Amish Life: Living Plainly and Serving God* (IUP, 2005), and *Invisible Presence* (IUP, 2006).

This book was designed by Jamison Cockerham and set in type by Tony Brewer at Indiana University Press and printed by Four Colour Imports, Ltd.

The text face is Arno, designed by Robert Slimbach, and the display face is Serlio, designed by the Linotype Design Studio, both issued by Adobe Systems.